Pontifical Council for J

The Social Agenda of the Catholic Church

A Collection of Magisterial Texts

With a foreword by

Archbishop François-Xavier Nguyễn Văn Thuận
President, Pontifical Council for Justice and Peace

Edited by

Rev. Robert A. Sirico
President, Acton Institute for the Study of Religion and Liberty
Grand Rapids, Michigan, USA

Rev. Maciej Zieba, O.P.
President, Instytut "Tertio Millennio"
Krakow, Poland

BURNS & OATES
A Continuum imprint
LONDON • NEW YORK

Burns & Oates
A Continuum imprint
The Tower Building
11 York Road
London SE1 7NX
www.continuumbooks.com

British Library Cataloguing-in-Publication Data
A catalogue record of this book is available from the British Library
ISBN 0 8264 6573 0

Typeset by BookEns Ltd, Royston, Herts
Printed and bound in Great Britain by Bookcraft (Bath) Ltd,
Midsomer Norton, Bath

CONTENTS

The Lord never abandons us. As I am writing this preface to a collection of texts on the social teaching of the Church, my mind goes back over fifty years to the year 1945. I was only seventeen years of age. My country, Vietnam, was at a moment of great difficulty. In many ways it had lost its way. Japan and Europe were shaken at the end of the war. Communism was making its inroads.

I was a young member of a small group of Catholics in the Imperial City of Huê. We were fortunate to have the texts of some of the social encyclicals, such as *Rerum Novarum, Quadragesimo Anno,* and *Divini Redemptoris.* In the face of great difficulties, we reproduced them as best we could.

One of our group—his name was Alexis—went from province to province bringing the texts to families and communities. He did so at enormous risk to himself and to his large family. At times, he would hide the texts by strapping them to his legs as he secretly moved from village to village. Finally, however, he was arrested and eventually died in prison.

But this work left behind a great legacy. So many young men and women found a new sense of hope through knowledge of the documents of the Church's social teaching. In fact, this knowledge opened up a *new path of light and hope* for them, which endured during the dark days that were to come. The Lord Jesus did not abandon them.

The Church's social teaching can have the same effect today in our situation that Pope Paul VI, in his final testament, called "dramatic and sad, yet magnificent." The social teaching of that remarkable series of Popes since Leo XIII can be, for the Christian of our time, a great source of orientation and a genuine instrument of evangelization. We all need this teaching.

In this Jubilee Year there have been many publications that bring together the various strands of Catholic social teaching. The *Catechism of the Catholic Church* contains many elements and is a most authoritative source. The Holy See is also preparing an authoritative synthesis of the social teaching of the Church, stressing its relationship with the "new evangelization." Other publications have recently emerged in Mexico and in Spain.

We celebrate the Jubilee Year as the anniversary of the Mystery of the Incarnation of Jesus Christ—God and man—who took on the human condition to redeem it. In a spirit of service to the celebration of the Great Jubilee of the Year 2000, the editors of this volume have brought together a useful collection of texts on the Church's social teaching. It will appear in seven languages and will be of great use for both academic and pastoral leaders, for political and business leaders, and, of course, for workers and the poor. I pray particularly that today those who represent the sufferings of the human condition will find through these texts the path to Jesus, our Redeemer, the only *new path of light and hope* for our time.

Like any collection, this publication does not claim to be complete. The individual texts have been selected because of their significance, but it is hoped that the reader will be led to re-read them in their full context and thus become more familiar with the breadth of Catholic social teaching.

Students, teachers, and all those who seek a better knowledge of the social doctrine of the Church will find contained within this collection the central statements of the Roman Pontiffs from a range of texts, including papal encyclicals, apostolic letters, and Conciliar documents, on matters relating to politics, economics, and culture. The selections are arranged thematically according to the significant subject areas of Catholic social doctrine. Under each subject heading, the quotations appear in pedagogical—as opposed to chronological or magisterial—order, with each subject area opening with a quotation that explains the issue at hand.

These statements have been offered from the heart of the Church to a world that so desperately needs a moral vision for constructing a more humane social order. While the Church does not pretend to offer scientific solutions to economic or social problems in the form of public-policy recommendations or precise legal prescriptions, what it does offer is far more important—a set of ideals and moral values that uphold and affirm the dignity of all. The application of such principles to economic, political, and social realities can result in justice and peace for all, genuine human development, and the liberation of people from oppression, poverty, and violence.

The Pontifical Council for Justice and Peace is grateful to the Reverend Robert A. Sirico and the Reverend Maciej Zieba, O.P., for editing this collection. The Pontifical Council also wishes to acknowledge the valuable assistance of the following persons in compiling the collection of texts: the staff of the Acton Institute for the Study of Religion and Liberty in Grand Rapids, Michigan, especially Gregory Gronbacher, Ph.D., Kevin Schmiesing, Ph.D., and Stephen J. Grabill, Th.M.; the Instytut "Tertio Millennio" in Krakow, especially Slawomir Sowinski and Piotr Kimla; the Very Reverend Professor Alvaro Corcuera Martínez del Río, L.C., Rector, the students and staff of the Pontificio Ateneo "Regina Apostolorum" in Rome; and the Reverend John-Peter Pham, S.T.D., Rome.

I am therefore pleased to commend this collection to all those who share our vision for the conjoining of justice and peace and to all who seek to know the Church's social teaching. I am especially satisfied to be able to offer this resource to teachers, theologians, catechists, and all those who instruct the faithful in the ways of truth. May the teaching of the Church's social doctrine contribute to the universal common good and help to establish the vision of the Psalmist in which justice and peace embrace (Ps 85:9–12), thus helping to usher in the Kingdom of God.

+ François-Xavier Nguyễn Văn Thuận
Titular Archbishop of Vadesi
President, Pontifical Council for Justice and Peace

Vatican City, 1 May 2000
Feast of Saint Joseph the Worker

ABBREVIATIONS*

CA   *Centesimus Annus* (On the Hundredth Anniversary of *Rerum Novarum*); John Paul II

CCC   *Catechism of the Catholic Church*

GS   *Gaudium et Spes* (Pastoral Constitution on the Church in the Modern World); Vatican Council II

LG   *Lumen Gentium* (Dogmatic Constitution on the Church); Vatican Council II

MM   *Mater et Magistra* (On Social Progress); John XXIII

PP   *Populorum Progressio* (On the Development of Peoples); Paul VI

PT   *Pacem in Terris* (Peace on Earth); John XXIII

QA   *Quadragesimo Anno* (On the Reconstruction of the Social Order); Pius XI

RN   *Rerum Novarum* (On the Condition of Workers); Leo XIII

SRS   *Sollicitudo Rei Socialis* (On Social Concern); John Paul II

TMA   *Tertio Millennio Adveniente* (On the Coming of the Third Millennium); John Paul II

*Only the documents appearing on this page have been marked in the collection with shortened title abbreviations. Full references to every other citation can be obtained by consulting the bibliography.

ARTICLE ONE

THE NATURE OF CATHOLIC
SOCIAL TEACHING

I. THE CHURCH AS MOTHER AND TEACHER

1. The Catholic Church has been established by Jesus Christ as mother and teacher of nations, so that all who in the course of centuries come to her loving embrace, may find salvation as well as the fullness of a more excellent life. To this Church, "the pillar and mainstay of the truth" (cf. 1 Tm 3:15), her most holy Founder has entrusted the double task of begetting sons unto herself, and of educating and governing those whom she begets, guiding with maternal providence the life both of individuals and of peoples. The lofty dignity of this life, she has always held in the highest respect and guarded with watchful care.
(*Mater et Magistra*, n. 1)

2. Doubtless, this most serious question demands the attention and the efforts of others besides ourselves—to wit, of the rulers of States, of employers of labor, of the wealthy, aye, of the working classes themselves, for whom We are pleading. But We affirm without hesitation that all the striving of men will be vain if they leave out the Church. Manifestly, it is the Church that draws from the Gospel the teachings through which the struggle can be composed entirely, or, after its bitterness is removed, can certainly become more tempered. It is the Church, again, that strives not only to instruct the mind but to regulate by her precepts the life and morals of individuals, that ameliorates the condition of the workers through her numerous and beneficent institutions, and that wishes and aims to have the thought and energy of all classes of society united to this end, that the interests of the workers be protected as fully as possible. To accomplish this purpose she holds that the laws and the authority of the State, within reasonable limits, ought to be obeyed.
(*Rerum Novarum*, n. 16)

3. For the teaching of Christ joins, as it were, earth with heaven, in that it embraces the whole man, namely, his soul and body, intellect and will, and bids him to lift up his mind from the changing conditions of human existence to that heavenly country where he will one day enjoy unending happiness and peace.
(*Mater et Magistra*, n. 2)

4. It is no wonder, then, that the Catholic Church, instructed by Christ and fulfilling his commands, has for two thousand years, from the ministry of the early deacons to the present time, tenaciously held aloft the torch of charity not only by her teaching but also by her widespread example—that charity which, by combining in a fitting manner the precepts and the practice of mutual love, puts into effect in a wonderful way this twofold commandment of giving, wherein is contained the full social teaching and action of the Church.
(*Mater et Magistra*, n. 6)

5. In light of the sacred teaching of the Second Vatican Council, the Church thus appears before us as the social subject of responsibility for divine truth. With deep emotion we hear Christ himself saying: "The word which you hear is not mine but the Father's who sent me" (Jn 14:24).... Therefore, it is required, when the Church professes and teaches the faith, that she should adhere strictly to divine truth (*Dei Verbum*, nn. 5, 10, 21), and should translate it into living attitudes of "obedience in harmony with reason" (cf. *Dei Filius*, chap. 3).
(*Redemptor Hominis*, n. 19)

6. In particular, as the Council affirms, *"the task of authentically interpreting the word of God, whether in its written form or in that of Tradition, has been entrusted only to those charged with the Church's living Magisterium, whose authority is exercised in the name*

of Jesus Christ" (*Dei Verbum*, n. 10). The Church, in her life and teaching, is thus revealed as "the pillar and bulwark of the truth" (1 Tm 3:15), including the truth regarding moral action. Indeed, "the Church has the right always and everywhere to proclaim moral principles, even in respect of the social order, and to make judgments about any human matter in so far as this is required by fundamental human rights or the salvation of souls" (*Code of Canon Law*, Canon 747, n. 2).

Precisely on the questions frequently debated in moral theology today and with regard to which new tendencies and theories have developed, the Magisterium, in fidelity to Jesus Christ and in continuity with the Church's Tradition, senses more urgently the duty to offer its own discernment and teaching, in order to help man in his journey toward truth and freedom.
(*Veritatis Splendor,* n. 27)

II. THE CHURCH'S MISSION

7. Coming forth from the eternal Father's love, founded in time by Christ the Redeemer and made one in the Holy Spirit, the Church has a saving and an eschatological purpose that can be fully attained only in the future world. But she is already present in this world, and is composed of men, that is, of members of the earthly city who have a call to form the family of God's children during the present history of the human race, and to keep increasing it until the Lord returns. United on behalf of heavenly values and enriched by them, this family has been "constituted and structured as a society in this world" (cf. Eph 1:3, 5:6, 13–14, 23) by Christ, and is equipped "by appropriate means for visible and social union." Thus the Church, at once "a visible association and a spiritual community" (LG, n. 8), goes forward together with humanity and experiences the same earthly lot

that the world does. She serves as a leaven and as a kind of soul for human society for its renewal in Christ and transformation into God's family.
(*Gaudium et Spes,* n. 40)

8. The teaching and spreading of her social doctrine are part of the Church's evangelizing mission. Since it is a doctrine aimed at guiding people's behavior, it consequently gives rise to a 'commitment to justice,' according to each individual's role, vocation, and circumstances.

The condemnation of evils and injustices is also part of that ministry of evangelization in the social field, which is an aspect of the Church's prophetic role. But it should be made clear that proclamation is always more important than condemnation, and the latter cannot ignore the former, which gives it true solidity and the force of higher motivation.
(*Sollicitudo Rei Socialis,* n. 41)

9. We profess our faith that the Kingdom of God, begun here below in the Church of Christ, is not of this world, whose form is passing away, and that its own growth cannot be confused with the progress of civilization, of science and of human technology, but that it consists in knowing ever more deeply the unfathomable riches of Christ, to hope ever more strongly in things eternal, to respond ever more ardently to the love of God, to spread ever more widely grace and holiness among men. But it is this very same love that makes the Church constantly concerned for the true temporal good of mankind as well. Never ceasing to recall to her children that they have no lasting dwelling here on earth, she urges them also to contribute, each according to his own vocation and means, to the welfare of their earthly city, to promote justice, peace and brotherhood among men, to lavish their assistance on their brothers, especially on

the poor and the most dispirited (cf. Paul VI, *Profession of Faith of the People of Libertatis Nuntius*, Conclusion *God,* n. 27).

10. Since it has been entrusted to the Church to reveal the mystery of God, Who is the ultimate goal of man, she opens up to man at the same time the meaning of his own existence, that is, the innermost truth about himself. The Church knows that only God, Whom she serves, meets the deepest longings of the human heart, which is never fully satisfied by what this world has to offer. (*Gaudium et Spes,* n. 41)

11. From this source the Church, equipped with the gifts of its Founder and faithfully guarding His precepts of charity, humility, and self-sacrifice, receives the mission to proclaim and to spread among all peoples the Kingdom of Christ and of God and to be, on earth, the initial budding forth of that kingdom. While it slowly grows, the Church strains toward the completed Kingdom and, with all its strength, hopes and desires to be united in glory with its King. (*Lumen Gentium,* n. 5)

12. As we know, the Church does not exist in isolation from the world. It lives in the world, and its members are consequently influenced and guided by the world. They imbibe its culture, are subject to its laws and adopt its customs. This intimate contact with the world is continually creating problems for the Church, and at the present time these problems are extremely acute.

The Christian life, as encouraged and preserved by the Church, must resist every possible source of deception, contamination, or restriction of its freedom. It must guard against these things as it would guard against contamination by error or evil. Yet at the same time it must not only adapt itself to the forms of thought and living which a temporal environment induces, one might almost say imposes,

on it—provided, of course, such forms are not incompatible with the basic principles of its religious and moral teaching—but it must also strive to approach these forms and to correct, ennoble, encourage, and sanctify them.
(*Ecclesiam Suam*, n. 42)

13. The Church offers mankind the Gospel, that prophetic message which responds to the needs and aspirations of the human heart and always remains 'Good News.' The Church cannot fail to proclaim that Jesus came to reveal the face of God and to merit salvation for all humanity by his cross and resurrection.
(*Redemptoris Missio*, n. 11)

14. All things human are our concern. We share with the whole of the human race a common nature, a common life, with all its gifts and all its problems. We are ready to play our part in this primary, universal society, to acknowledge the insistent demands of its fundamental needs, and to applaud the new and often sublime expressions of its genius. But there are moral values of the utmost importance which we have to offer it. These are of advantage to everyone. We root them firmly in the consciences of men. Wherever men are striving to understand themselves and the world, we are able to communicate with them.
(*Ecclesiam Suam*, n. 97)

III. THE CHURCH'S SOCIAL MESSAGE

15. The social concern of the Church, directed toward an authentic development of man and society that would respect and promote all the dimensions of the human person, has always expressed itself in the most varied ways. In recent years, one of the special

means of intervention has been the Magisterium of the Roman Pontiffs which, beginning with the encyclical *Rerum Novarum* of Leo XIII as a point of reference, has frequently dealt with the question and has sometimes made the dates of publication of the various social documents coincide with the anniversaries of that first document. The Popes have not failed to throw fresh light by means of those messages upon new aspects of the social doctrine of the Church. As a result, this doctrine, beginning with the outstanding contribution of Leo XIII and enriched by the successive contributions of the Magisterium, has now become an updated doctrinal 'corpus.' It builds up gradually, as the Church, in the fullness of the word revealed by Christ Jesus (cf. *Dei Verbum*, n. 4) and with the assistance of the Holy Spirit (cf. Jn 14:16, 26; 16:13–15), reads events as they unfold in the course of history. She thus seeks to lead people to respond, with the support also of rational reflection and of the human sciences, to their vocation as responsible builders of earthly society. (*Sollicitudo Rei Socialis,* n. 1)

16. Amid the disturbances and uncertainties of the present hour, the Church has a specific message to proclaim and a support to give to men in their efforts to take in hand and give direction to their futures. Since the period in which the encyclical *Rerum Novarum* denounced in a forceful and imperative manner the scandal of the condition of the workers in the nascent industrial society, historical evolution has led to an awareness of other dimensions and other applications of social justice. The encyclicals *Quadragesimo Anno* and *Mater et Magistra* already noted this fact. The recent Council for its part took care to point them out, in particular in the Pastoral Constitution *Gaudium et Spes*. We ourselves have already continued these lines of thought in our encyclical *Populorum Progressio*, "Today," we said, "the principal fact that we must all recognize is that the social question has become worldwide" (PP, n. 3). A renewed con-

sciousness of the demands of the gospel makes it the Church's duty to put herself at the service of all, to help them grasp their serious problem in all its dimensions, and to convince them that solidarity in actions at this turning point in human history is a matter of urgency.
(*Octogesima Adveniens*, n. 5)

17. "Christian revelation ... promotes deeper understanding of the laws of social living" (GS, n. 23). The Church receives from the Gospel the full revelation of the truth about man. When she fulfills her mission of proclaiming the Gospel, she bears witness to man, in the name of Christ, to his dignity and his vocation to the communion of persons. She teaches him the demands of justice and peace in conformity with divine wisdom.
(CCC, n. 2419)

18. The social doctrine of the Church, which proposes a set of principles for reflection, criteria for judgment and directives for action is addressed in the first place to members of the Church. It is essential that the faithful engaged in human promotion should have a firm grasp of this precious body of teaching and make it an integral part of their evangelizing mission.... Christian leaders in the Church and society, and especially lay men and women with responsibilities in public life, need to be well formed in this teaching so that they can inspire and vivify civil society and its structures with the leaven of the Gospel.
(*Ecclesia in Asia*, n. 32)

19. The situation today points to an ever-increasing urgency for a doctrinal formation of the lay faithful, not simply in a better understanding which is natural to faith's dynamism, but also in enabling them 'to give a reason for their hoping' in view of the world and its grave and complex problems.... This is especially true for the lay

faithful who have responsibilities in various fields of society and public life. Above all, it is indispensable that they have a more exact knowledge—and this demands a more widespread and precise presentation—of the Church's social doctrine, as repeatedly stressed by the Synod Fathers in their presentations.
(*Christifideles Laici*, n. 60)

20. True to the teaching and example of her divine Founder, Who cited the preaching of the Gospel to the poor as a sign of His mission (cf. Lk 7:22), the Church has never failed to foster the human progress of the nations to which she brings faith in Christ.
(*Populorum Progressio*, n. 12)

21. *The Church shares with the people of our time* this profound and ardent desire for a life which is just in every aspect, nor does she fail to examine the various aspects of the sort of justice that the life of people and society demands. This is confirmed by the field of Catholic social doctrine, greatly developed in the course of the last century. On the lines of this teaching proceed the education and formation of human consciences in the spirit of justice, and also of the apostolate of the laity, which are developing in precisely this spirit. And yet, it would be difficult not to notice that very often *programs which start from the idea of justice* and which ought to assist its fulfillment among individuals, groups and human socities, *in practice suffer from distortions*.
(*Dives in Misericordia*, n. 12)

22. If, as We said, the Church realizes what is God's will in its regard, it will gain for itself a great store of energy, and in addition will conceive the need for pouring out this energy in the service of all men. It will have a clear awareness of a mission received from God, of a message to be spread far and wide. Here lies the source of our evan-

gelical duty, our mandate to teach all nations, and our apostolic endeavor to strive for the eternal salvation of all men.
(*Ecclesiam Suam*, n. 64)

23. To be sure, there is no single model for organizing the politics and economics of human freedom; different cultures and different historical experiences give rise to different institutional forms of public life in a free and responsible society.
(*Address to the Fiftieth General Assembly of the United Nations Organization*, 1995, n. 3)

24. In addition, the Church's social teaching has an important interdisciplinary dimension. In order better to incarnate the one truth about man in different and constantly changing social, economic and political contexts, this teaching enters into dialogue with the various disciplines concerned with man. It assimilates what these disciplines have to contribute, and helps them to open themselves to a broader horizon, aimed at serving the individual person who is acknowledged and loved in the fullness of his or her vocation. Parallel with the interdisciplinary aspect, mention should also be made of the practical and, as it were, experiential dimension of this teaching, which is to be found at the crossroads where Christian life and conscience come into contact with the real world. This teaching is seen in the efforts of individuals, families, people involved in cultural and social life, as well as politicians and statesmen to give it a concrete form and application in history.
(*Centesimus Annus*, n. 59)

IV. THE SCOPE OF THE CHURCH'S SOCIAL TEACHING

25. The Church has no models to present; models that are real and truly effective can only arise within the framework of different historical situations, through the efforts of all those who responsibly confront concrete problems in all their social, economic, political and cultural aspects, as these interact with one another (cf. GS, n. 36; *Octogesima Adveniens*, nn. 2–5). For such a task the Church offers her social teaching as an indispensable and ideal orientation, a teaching which, as already mentioned, recognizes the positive value of the market and of enterprise, but which at the same time points out that these must be oriented toward the common good.
(*Centesimus Annus*, n. 43)

26. The Church's social teaching comprises a body of doctrine, which is articulated as the Church interprets events in the course of history, with the assistance of the Holy Spirit, in the light of the whole of what has been revealed by Jesus Christ (SRS, n. 1). This teaching can be more easily accepted by men of good will; the more the faithful let themselves be guided by it.
(CCC, n. 2422)

27. However, when it comes to reducing these teachings to action, it sometimes happens that even sincere Catholic men have differing views. When this occurs, they should take care to have and to show mutual esteem and regard, and to explore the extent to which they can work in cooperation among themselves. Thus they can in good time accomplish what necessity required. Let them also take great care not to weaken their efforts in constant controversies. Nor should they, under pretext of seeking what they think best, meanwhile fail to do what they can and hence should do.
(*Mater et Magistra,* n. 238)

28. The Church has no philosophy of her own, nor does she canonize any one particular philosophy in preference to others. The underlying reason for this reluctance is that, even when it engages theology, philosophy must remain faithful to its own principles and methods. Otherwise there would be no guarantee that it would remain oriented to truth and that it was moving toward truth by way of a process governed by reason. A philosophy that did not proceed in the light of reason according to its own principles and methods would serve little purpose. At the deepest level, the autonomy that philosophy enjoys is rooted in the fact that reason is by its nature oriented to truth and is equipped moreover with the means necessary to arrive at truth. A philosophy conscious of this as its 'constitutive status' cannot but respect the demands and the data of revealed truth.
(*Fides et Ratio*, n. 49)

29. The social doctrine of the Church developed in the nineteenth century when the Gospel encountered modern industrial society with its new structures for the production of consumer goods, its new concept of society, the state, and authority, and its new forms of labor and ownership. The development of the doctrine of the Church on economic and social matters attests to the permanent value of the Church's teaching at the same time as it attests to the true meaning of her Tradition, always living and active (cf. CA, n. 3).
(CCC, n. 2421)

30. The Church's social doctrine is not a 'third way' between liberal capitalism and Marxist collectivism, nor even a possible alternative to other solutions less radically opposed to one another: rather, it constitutes a category of its own. Nor is it an ideology, but rather the accurate formulation of the results of a careful reflection on the complex realities of human existence, in society and in the international order, in the light of faith and of the Church's tradition.

Its main aim is to interpret these realities, determining their conformity with or divergence from the lines of the Gospel teaching on man and his vocation, a vocation that is at once earthly and transcendent; its aim is thus to guide Christian behavior. It therefore belongs to the field, not of ideology, but of theology and particularly of moral theology.
(*Sollicitudo Rei Socialis*, n. 41)

31. Certainly the Church was not given the commission to guide men to a fleeting and perishable happiness but to that which is eternal. Indeed, the Church holds that "it is unlawful for her to mix without cause in these temporal concerns"; (*Ubi Arcano Dei Consilio*, n. 65) however, she can in no wise renounce the duty God entrusted to her to interpose her authority, not of course in matters of technique for which she is neither suitably equipped nor endowed by office, but in all things that are connected with the moral law. For as to these, the deposit of truth that God committed to us and the grave duty of disseminating and interpreting the whole moral law, and of urging it in season and out of season, bring under and subject to our supreme jurisdiction not only social order but economic activities themselves.
(*Quadragesimo Anno*, n. 41)

32. Today, the Church's social doctrine focuses especially on man as he is involved in a complex network of relationships within modern societies. The human sciences and philosophy are helpful for interpreting man's central place within society and for enabling him to understand himself better as a social being. However, man's true identity is only fully revealed to him through faith, and it is precisely from faith that the Church's social teaching begins.
(*Centesimus Annus*, n. 54)

15

V. EVANGELIZATION AND CHURCH SOCIAL TEACHING

33. The 'new evangelization,' which the modern world urgently needs and which I have emphasized many times, must include among its essential elements *a proclamation of the Church's social doctrine*. As in the days of Pope Leo XIII, this doctrine is still suitable for indicating the right way to respond to the great challenges of today, when ideologies are being increasingly discredited. Now, as then, we need to repeat that there can be *no genuine solution of the 'social question' apart from the Gospel*, and that the 'new things' can find in the Gospel the context for their correct understanding and the proper moral perspective for judgment on them.
(*Centesimus Annus,* n. 5)

34. What counts, here as in every area of Christian life, is the confidence that comes from faith, from the certainty that it is not we who are the principal agents of the Church's mission, but Jesus Christ and his Spirit. We are only co-workers, and when we have done all that we can, we must say: "We are unworthy servants; we have only done our duty" (Lk 17:10).
(*Redemptoris Missio,* n. 36)

35. I now wish to propose a 'rereading' of Pope Leo's encyclical by issuing an invitation to 'look back' at the text itself in order to discover anew the richness of the fundamental principles which it formulated for dealing with the question of the condition of workers....
A rereading of this kind will not only confirm the permanent value of such teaching, but will also manifest the true meaning of the Church's Tradition which, being ever living and vital, builds upon the foundation laid by our fathers in the faith, and particularly upon what "the Apostles passed down to the Church" (St. Irenaeus,

Adversus Haereses, I, 10) in the name of Jesus Christ, who is her irreplaceable foundation (cf. 1 Cor 3:11).
(*Centesimus Annus*, n. 3)

36. The presentation of the Gospel message is not an optional contribution for the Church. It is the duty incumbent on her by the command of the Lord Jesus, so that people can believe and be saved. This message is indeed necessary. It is unique. It cannot be replaced.
(*Evangelii Nuntiandi*, n. 5)

37. *We have been sent.* For us, being at the service of life is not a boast but rather a duty, born of our awareness of being "God's own people, that we may declare the wonderful deeds of him who called us out of darkness into his marvellous light" (cf. 1 Pt 2:9). On our journey *we are guided and sustained by the law of love*: a love which has as its source and model the Son of God made man, who "by dying gave life to the world" (cf. Roman Missal, Prayer Before Communion).

We have been sent as a people. Everyone has an obligation to be at the service of life. This is a properly 'ecclesial' responsibility, which requires concerted and generous action by all the members and by all sectors of the Christian community. This community commitment does not, however, eliminate or lessen the responsibility of each *individual,* called by the Lord to "become the neighbour" of everyone: "Go and do likewise" (Lk 10:37).
(*Evangelium Vitae*, n. 79)

38. Together we all sense our duty to *preach the Gospel of life,* to *celebrate it* in the Liturgy and in our whole existence, and to *serve it* with the various programs and structures which support and promote life.
(*Evangelium Vitae,* n. 79)

ARTICLE TWO

THE HUMAN PERSON

I. THE DIGNITY OF THE HUMAN PERSON

39. In effect, to teach and to spread her social doctrine pertains to the Church's evangelizing mission and is an essential part of the Christian message, since this doctrine points out the direct consequences of that message in the life of society and situates daily work and struggles for justice in the context of bearing witness to Christ the Savior. This doctrine is likewise a source of unity and peace in dealing with the conflicts which inevitably arise in social and economic life. Thus it is possible to meet these new situations without degrading the human person's transcendent dignity, either in oneself or in one's adversaries, and to direct those situations toward just solutions.
(*Centesimus Annus*, n. 5)

40. This is why the Church has something to say today, just as twenty years ago, and also in the future, about the nature, conditions, requirements and aims of authentic development, and also about the obstacles which stand in its way. In doing so the Church fulfills her mission to evangelize, for she offers her first contribution to the solution of the urgent problem of development when she proclaims the truth about Christ, about herself and about man, applying this truth to a concrete situation (cf. John Paul II, *Address to Latin American Bishops*, 1979).

As her instrument for reaching this goal, the Church uses her social doctrine. In today's difficult situation, a more exact awareness and a wider diffusion of the "set of principles for reflection, criteria for judgment and directives for action" proposed by the Church's teaching (*Libertatis Conscientia*, n. 72; *Octogesima Adveniens*, n. 4) would be of great help in promoting both the correct definition of the problems being faced and the best solution to them.

It will thus be seen at once that the questions facing us are above

all moral questions; and that neither the analysis of the problem of development as such nor the means to overcome the present difficulties can ignore this essential dimension.
(*Sollicitudo Rei Socialis*, n. 41)

41. In the life of man, God's image shines forth anew and is again revealed in all its fullness at the coming of the Son of God in human flesh. "Christ is the image of the invisible God" (Col 1:15); he "reflects the glory of God and bears the very stamp of his nature" (Heb 1:3). He is the perfect image of the Father.
(*Evangelium Vitae*, n. 36)

42. The dignity of the person is manifested in all its radiance when the person's origin and destiny are considered: created by God in his image and likeness as well as redeemed by the most precious blood of Christ, the person is called to be a 'child in the Son' and a living temple of the Spirit, destined for eternal life of blessed communion with God. For this very reason every violation of the personal dignity of the human being cries out in vengeance to God and is an offense against the Creator of the individual.
(*Christifideles Laici*, n. 37)

43. If we look upon the dignity of the human person in the light of divinely revealed truth, we cannot help but esteem it far more highly; for men are redeemed by the blood of Jesus Christ, they are by grace the children and friends of God and heirs of eternal glory.
(*Pacem in Terris*, n. 10)

44. Thanks to this belief, the Church can anchor the dignity of human nature against all tides of opinion, for example, those that undervalue the human body or idolize it. By no human law can the personal dignity and liberty of man be so aptly safeguarded as by the

Gospel of Christ that has been entrusted to the Church. For this Gospel announces and proclaims the freedom of the sons of God, and repudiates all the bondage that ultimately results from sin (cf. Rom 8:14–17). It has a sacred reverence for the dignity of conscience and its freedom of choice, constantly advises that all human talents be employed in God's service and men's, and, finally, commends all to the charity of all (cf. Mt 22:39). This agrees with the basic law of the Christian dispensation. For though the same God is Savior and Creator, Lord of human history as well as of salvation history, in the divine arrangement itself, the rightful autonomy of the creature, and particularly of man is not withdrawn, but is rather reestablished in its own dignity and strengthened. The Church, therefore, by virtue of the Gospel committed to her, proclaims the rights of man; she acknowledges and greatly esteems the dynamic movements of today by which these rights are everywhere fostered. Yet these movements must be penetrated by the spirit of the Gospel and protected against any kind of false autonomy. For we are tempted to think that our personal rights are fully ensured only when we are exempt from every requirement of divine law. But in this way lies not the maintenance of the dignity of the human person but its annihilation.
(*Gaudium et Spes*, n. 41)

45. At stake is the *dignity of the human person*, whose *defense* and *promotion* have been entrusted to us by the Creator, and to whom the men and women at every moment of history are strictly and responsibly in debt.
(*Sollicitudo Rei Socialis*, n. 47)

46. The dignity of the human person is a transcendent value, always recognized as such by those who sincerely search for the truth. Indeed, the whole of human history should be interpreted in the light of this certainty. Every person, created in the image and likeness of

God (cf. Gn 1:26–28), is therefore radically oriented towards the Creator, and is constantly in relationship with those possessed of the same dignity. To promote the good of the individual is thus to serve the common good, which is that point where rights and duties converge and reinforce one another.
(*World Day of Peace Message*, 1999, n. 2)

47. "Where the Spirit of the Lord is, there is freedom" (2 Cor 3:17). This revelation of freedom and hence of man's true dignity acquires a particular eloquence for Christians and for the Church in a state of persecution—both in ancient times and in the present—because the witnesses to divine Truth then become a living proof of the action of the Spirit of truth present in the hearts and minds of the faithful, and they often mark with their own death by martyrdom the supreme glorification of human dignity.
(*Dominum et Vivificantem,* n. 60)

II. Freedom and Truth

48. The question of morality, to which Christ provides the answer, cannot prescind from the issue of freedom. Indeed, it considers that issue central, for there can be no morality without freedom: "It is only in freedom that man can turn to what is good" (GS, n. 11). But what sort of freedom? The Council, considering our contemporaries who "highly regard" freedom and "assiduously pursue" it, but who "often cultivate it in wrong ways as a license to do anything they please, even evil," speaks of 'genuine' freedom: "Genuine freedom is an outstanding manifestation of the divine image in man. For God willed to leave man 'in the power of his own counsel' (cf. Sir 15:14), so that he would seek his Creator of his own accord and would freely arrive at full and blessed perfection by cleaving to God" (GS,

n. 17). Although each individual has a right to be respected in his own journey in search of the truth, there exists a prior moral obligation, and a grave one at that, to seek the truth and to adhere to it once it is known.
(*Veritatis Splendor*, n. 34)

49. Freedom in its essence is within man, is connatural to the human person and is the distinctive sign of man's nature. The freedom of the individual finds its basis in man's transcendent dignity: a dignity given to him by God, his Creator, and which directs him toward God. Because he has been created in God's image (cf. Gn 1:27), man is inseparable from freedom, that freedom which no external force or constraint can ever take away, and which constitutes his fundamental right, both as an individual and as a member of society. Man is free because he possesses the faculty of self-determination with regard to what is true and what is good.
(*World Day of Peace Message*, 1981, n. 5)

50. Jesus Christ meets the man of every age, including our own, with the same words: "You will know the truth and the truth will make you free" (Jn 8:32). These words contain both a fundamental requirement and a warning: the requirement of an honest relationship with regard to truth as a condition for authentic freedom, and the warning to avoid every kind of illusory freedom, every superficial unilateral freedom, every freedom that fails to enter into the truth about man and the whole world.
(*Redemptor Hominis*, n. 12)

51. But freedom is not merely a right that one claims for oneself. It is also a duty that one undertakes with regard to others. If it is really to serve peace, the freedom of each human individual and each community must respect the freedoms and rights of other individuals

and communities. This respect sets a limit to freedom, but it also gives it its logic and dignity, since we are by nature social beings. (*World Day of Peace Message*, 1981, n. 7)

52. The exercise of freedom does not imply a right to say or to do everything. It is false to maintain that man, "the subject of this freedom," is "an individual who is fully self-sufficient and whose finality is the satisfaction of his own interests in the enjoyment of earthly goods" (*Libertatis Conscientia,* n. 13). Moreover, the economic, social, political, and cultural conditions that are needed for a just exercise of freedom are too often disregarded or violated. Such situations of blindness and injustice injure the moral life and involve the strong as well as the weak in the temptation to sin against charity. By deviating from the moral law, man violates his own freedom, becomes imprisoned within himself, disrupts neighborly fellowship, and rebels against divine truth.
(CCC, n. 1740)

53. But the Creator of the world has imprinted in man's heart an order that his conscience reveals to him and enjoins him to obey: This shows that the obligations of the law are written in their hearts; their conscience utters its own testimony (Rm 2:15). And how could it be otherwise? For whatever God has made shows forth His infinite wisdom, and it is manifested more clearly in the things that have greater perfection (cf. Ps 18:8–11).
(*Pacem in Terris,* n. 5)

54. In the design of God, every man is called upon to develop and fulfill himself, for every life is a vocation. At birth, everyone is granted, in germ, a set of aptitudes and qualities for him to bring to fruition. Their coming to maturity, which will be the result of education received from the environment and personal efforts, will allow

each man to direct himself toward the destiny intended for him by the Creator. Endowed with intelligence and freedom, he is responsible for his fulfillment as he is for his salvation. He is aided, or sometimes impeded, by those who educate him and those with whom he lives, but each one remains, whatever these influences affecting him might be, the principal agent of his own success or failure. By the unaided effort of his own intelligence and his will, each man can grow in humanity, can enhance his personal worth, can become more a person.
(*Populorum Progressio,* n. 15)

55. In the end, when He completed on the cross the work of redemption whereby He achieved salvation and true freedom for men, He also brought his revelation to completion. He bore witness to the truth, but He refused to impose the truth by force on those who spoke against it. Not by force of blows does his rule assert its claims. Rather, it is established by witnessing to the truth and by hearing the truth, and it extends its dominion by the love whereby Christ, lifted up on the cross, draws all men to Himself (cf. Jn 12:32).
(*Dignitatis Humanae,* n. 11)

56. Finally, true freedom is not advanced in the permissive society, which confuses freedom with license to do anything whatever, and which, in the name of freedom, proclaims a kind of general amorality. It is a caricature of freedom to claim that people are free to organize their lives with no reference to moral values, and to say that society does not have to ensure the protection and advancement of ethical values. Such an attitude is destructive of freedom and peace.
(*World Day of Peace Message,* 1981, n. 7)

57. Nor does the Church close her eyes to the danger of fanaticism or fundamentalism among those who, in the name of an ideology

which purports to be scientific or religious, claim the right to impose on others their own concept of what is true and good. Christian truth is not of this kind. Since it is not an ideology, the Christian faith does not presume to imprison changing socio-political realities in a rigid schema, and it recognizes that human life is realized in history in conditions that are diverse and imperfect. Furthermore, in constantly affirming the transcendent dignity of the person, the Church's method is always that of respect for freedom.
(*Centesimus Annus*, n. 46)

58. Democracy cannot be sustained without a shared commitment to certain moral truths about the human person and the human community. The basic question before a democratic society is: "How ought we live together?" In seeking an answer to this question, can society exclude moral truth and moral reasoning?....

Every generation ... needs to know that freedom consists not in doing what we like, but in having the right to do what we ought.

Christ asks us to guard the truth because, as he promised us: "You will know the truth and the truth will make you free." *Depositum custodi!* We must guard the truth that is the authentic condition of freedom, the truth that allows freedom to be fulfilled in goodness. We must guard the deposit of divine truth handed down to us in the Church, especially in view of the challenges posed by a materialistic culture and by a permissive society that reduces freedom to license.
(John Paul II, Homily in Baltimore, nn. 7–8)

59. While these [conditions] certainly have an influence on freedom, they do not determine it; they make the exercise of freedom more difficult or less difficult, but they cannot destroy it. Not only is it wrong from the ethical point of view to disregard human nature, which is made for freedom, but in practice it is impossible to do so.

Where society is so organized as to reduce arbitrarily or even suppress the sphere in which freedom is legitimately exercised, the result is that the life of society becomes progressively disorganized and goes into decline.
(*Centesimus Annus*, n. 25)

III. THE SOCIAL NATURE OF MAN

60. God, Who has fatherly concern for everyone, has willed that all men should constitute one family and treat one another in a spirit of brotherhood. For having been created in the image of God, Who "from one man has created the whole human race and made them live all over the face of the earth" (Acts 17:26), all men are called to one and the same goal, namely God Himself. For this reason, love for God and neighbor is the first and greatest commandment. Sacred Scripture, however, teaches us that the love of God cannot be separated from the love of neighbor: "If there is any other commandment, it is summed up in this saying: Thou shalt love thy neighbor as thyself.... Love therefore is the fulfillment of the Law" (Rom 13:9–10; cf. 1 Jn 4:20). To men growing daily more dependent on one another, and to a world becoming more unified every day, this truth proves to be of paramount importance. Indeed, the Lord Jesus, when He prayed to the Father, "that all may be one ... as we are one" (Jn 17:21–22), opened up vistas closed to human reason, for He implied a certain likeness between the union of the divine Persons, and the unity of God's sons in truth and charity. This likeness reveals that man, who is the only creature on earth that God willed for itself, cannot fully find himself except through a sincere gift of himself.

Man's social nature makes it evident that the progress of the human person and the advance of society itself hinge on one another. For the beginning, the subject and the goal of all social institutions is

and must be the human person that for its part and by its very nature stands completely in need of social life. Since this social life is not something added on to man, through his dealings with others, through reciprocal duties, and through fraternal dialogue he develops all his gifts and is able to rise to his destiny.
(*Gaudium et Spes,* nn. 24–25)

61. The cardinal point of this teaching is that individual men are necessarily the foundation, cause, and end of all social institutions. We are referring to human beings, insofar as they are naturally social, and raised to an order of existence that transcends and subdues nature.
(*Mater et Magistra*, n. 219)

62. Certain societies, such as the family and the state, correspond more directly to the nature of man; they are necessary to him. To promote the participation of the greatest number in the life of a society, the creation of voluntary associations and institutions must be encouraged "on both national and international levels, which relate to economic and social goals, to cultural and recreational activities, to sport, to various professions, and to political affairs" (MM, n. 60). This 'socialization' also expresses the natural tendency for human beings to associate with one another for the sake of attaining objectives that exceed individual capacities. It develops the qualities of the person, especially the sense of initiative and responsibility, and helps guarantee his rights (GS, n. 25; CA, n. 12).
(CCC, n. 1882)

63. But each man is a member of society. He is part of the whole of mankind. It is not just certain individuals, but all men who are called to this fullness of development. Civilizations are born, develop, and die. But humanity is advancing along the path of history like

the waves of a rising tide encroaching gradually on the shore. We have inherited from past generations, and we have benefited from the work of our contemporaries: for this reason we have obligations toward all, and we cannot refuse to interest ourselves in those who will come after us to enlarge the human family. The reality of human solidarity, which is a benefit for us, also imposes a duty. (*Populorum Progressio*, n. 17)

64. Apart from the family, other intermediate communities exercise primary functions and give life to specific networks of solidarity. These develop as real communities of persons and strengthen the social fabric, preventing society from becoming an anonymous and impersonal mass, as unfortunately often happens today. It is in interrelationships on many levels that a person lives, and that society becomes more 'personalized.' The individual today is often suffocated between two poles represented by the State and the marketplace. At times it seems as though he exists only as a producer and consumer of goods, or as an object of state administration. People lose sight of the fact that life in society has neither the market nor the State as its final purpose, since life itself has a unique value that the State and the market must serve. Man remains above all a being who seeks the truth and strives to live in that truth, deepening his understanding of it through a dialogue involving past and future generations. (*Centesimus Annus*, n. 49)

65. In contrast, from the Christian vision of the human person there necessarily follows a correct picture of society. According to *Rerum Novarum* and the whole social doctrine of the Church, the social nature of man is not completely fulfilled in the State, but is realized in various intermediary groups, beginning with the family and including economic, social, political and cultural groups which stem from human nature itself and have their own autonomy, always

with a view to the common good. This is what I have called the "sub-jectivity" of society which, together with the subjectivity of the individual, was cancelled out by "Real Socialism" (SRS, nn. 15, 28). (*Centesimus Annus*, n. 13)

IV. HUMAN RIGHTS

66. Beginning our discussion of the rights of man, we see that every man has the right to life, to bodily integrity, and to the means suitable for the proper development of life; these are primarily food, clothing, shelter, rest, medical care, and, finally, the necessary social services. Therefore, a human being also has the right to security in cases of sickness, inability to work, widowhood, old age, unemploy-ment, or in any other case in which he is deprived of the means of subsistence through no fault of his own.
(*Pacem in Terris,* n. 11)

67. Following the collapse of Communist totalitarianism and of many other totalitarian and 'national security' regimes, today we are witnessing a predominance, not without signs of opposition, of the democratic ideal, together with lively attention to and concern for human rights. But for this very reason it is necessary for peoples in the process of reforming their systems to give democracy an authen-tic and solid foundation through the explicit recognition of those rights (cf. *Redemptor Hominis*, n. 17).
(*Centesimus Annus*, n. 47)

68. Any human society, if it is to be well-ordered and produc-tive, must lay down as a foundation this principle, namely, that every human being is a person, that is, his nature is endowed with intelli-gence and free will. Indeed, precisely because he is a person, he has

rights and obligations flowing directly and simultaneously from his very nature. And as these rights and obligations are universal and inviolable, so they cannot in any way be surrendered.
(*Pacem in Terris*, n. 9)

69. After all, peace comes down to respect for man's inviolable rights ... while war springs from the violation of these rights and brings with it still graver violations of them. If human rights are violated in a time of peace, this is particularly painful and, from the point of view of progress, it represents an incomprehensible manifestation of activity directed against man, which can in no way be reconciled with any program that describes itself as humanistic.
(*Redemptor Hominis*, n. 17)

70. The human person is also entitled to a juridical protection of his rights, a protection that should be efficacious, impartial, and inspired by the true norms of justice. As Our Predecessor Pius XII teaches: "That perpetual privilege proper to man, by which every individual has a claim to the protection of his rights, and by which there is assigned to each a definite and particular sphere of rights immune from all arbitrary attacks, is the logical consequence of the order of justice willed by God" (Pius XII, Christmas Eve Radio Message, 1942).
(*Pacem in Terris*, n. 27)

71. Respect for the human person entails respect for the rights that flow from his dignity as a creature. These rights are prior to society and must be recognized by it. They are the basis of the moral legitimacy of every authority: by flouting them, or refusing to recognize them in its positive legislation, a society undermines its own moral legitimacy (cf. PT, n. 65). If it does not respect them, authority can rely only on force or violence to obtain obedience from its subjects.

It is the Church's role to remind men of good will of these rights and
to distinguish them from unwarranted or false claims.
(CCC, n. 1930)

72. When the relations of human society are expressed in terms
of rights and duties, men become conscious of spiritual values, understand the meaning and significance of truth, justice, charity, freedom, and become deeply aware that they belong to this world of
values. Moreover, when moved by such concerns, they are
brought to a better knowledge of the true God Who is personal and
transcendent, and thus they make the ties that bind them to God the
solid foundation and supreme criterion of their lives, both of that life
which they live interiorly in the depths of their own souls and of that
in which they are united to other men in society.
(*Pacem in Terris*, n. 45)

73. Although private societies exist within the State and are, as
it were, so many parts of it, still it is not within the authority of the
State universally and *per se* to forbid them to exist as such. For man
is permitted by a right of nature to form private societies; the State,
on the other hand, has been instituted to protect and not to destroy
natural right, and if it should forbid its citizens to enter into associations, it would clearly do something contradictory to itself because
both the State itself and private associations are begotten of one and
the same principle, namely, that men are by nature inclined to associate.
(*Rerum Novarum*, n. 51)

74. In human society, to one man's right, there corresponds a
duty in all other persons: the duty, namely, of acknowledging and
respecting the right in question. For every fundamental human right
draws its indestructible moral force from the natural law, which, in

granting it, imposes a corresponding obligation. Those, therefore, who claim their own rights, yet altogether forget or neglect to carry out their respective duties, are people who build with one hand and destroy with the other.
(*Pacem in Terris,* n. 30)

75. On the contrary, the conviction that all men are equal by reason of their natural dignity has been generally accepted. Hence, racial discrimination can in no way be justified, at least doctrinally or in theory. And this is of fundamental importance and significance for the formation of human society according to those principles that we have outlined above. For, if a man becomes conscious of his rights, he must become equally aware of his duties. Thus, he who possesses certain rights has likewise the duty to claim those rights as marks of his dignity, while all others have the obligation to acknowledge those rights and respect them.
(*Pacem in Terris*, n. 44)

76. Since all men possess a rational soul and are created in God's likeness, since they have the same nature and origin, have been redeemed by Christ and enjoy the same divine calling and destiny, the basic equality of all must receive increasingly greater recognition.

True, all men are not alike from the point of view of varying physical power and the diversity of intellectual and moral resources. Nevertheless, with respect to the fundamental rights of the person, every type of discrimination, whether social or cultural, whether based on sex, race, color, social condition, language, or religion, is to be overcome and eradicated as contrary to God's intent. For in truth it must be regretted that fundamental personal rights are still not being universally honored. Such is the case of a woman who is denied the right to choose a husband freely, to embrace a state of life, or to acquire an education or cultural benefits equal to those recognized for men.

Therefore, although rightful differences exist between men, the equal dignity of persons demands that a more humane and just condition of life be brought about. For excessive economic and social differences between the members of the one human family or population groups cause scandal, and militate against social justice, equity, the dignity of the human person, as well as social and international peace.

Human institutions, both private and public, must labor to minister to the dignity and purpose of man. At the same time, let them put up a stubborn fight against any kind of slavery, whether social or political, and safeguard the basic rights of man under every political system. Indeed, human institutions themselves must be accommodated by degrees to the highest of all realities, spiritual ones, even though meanwhile, a long enough time will be required before they arrive at the desired goal.
(*Gaudium et Spes*, n. 29)

77. The necessity of ensuring fundamental human rights cannot be separated from this just liberation which is bound up with evangelization and which endeavors to secure structures safeguarding human freedoms. Among these fundamental human rights, religious liberty occupies a place of primary importance.
(*Evangelii Nuntiandi*, n. 39)

V. RELIGIOUS FREEDOM

78. This Vatican synod declares that the human person has a right to religious freedom. This freedom means that all men are to be immune from coercion on the part of individuals or social groups and of any human power, in such wise that in matters religious no one is to be forced to act in a manner contrary to his own beliefs.

Nor is anyone to be restrained from acting in accordance with his own beliefs, whether privately or publicly, whether alone or in association with others, within due limits.
(*Dignitatis Humanae*, n. 2)

79. Certainly the curtailment of religious freedom of individuals and communities is not only a painful experience, but it is above all an attack on man's very dignity, independently of the religion professed or the concept of the world which these individuals and communities have. The curtailment and violation of religious freedom are in contrast with man's dignity and his objective rights.... In this case we are undoubtedly confronted with a radical injustice with regard to what is particularly deep within man, what is authentically human.
(*Redemptor Hominis*, n. 17)

80. No human authority has the right to interfere with a person's conscience. Conscience bears witness to the transcendence of the person, also in regard to society at large, and, as such, is inviolable. Conscience, however, is not an absolute placed above truth and error. Rather, by its very nature, it implies a relation to objective truth, a truth which is universal, the same for all, which all can and must seek. It is in relation to objective truth that freedom of conscience finds its justification, inasmuch as it is a necessary condition for seeking truth worthy of man, and for adhering to that truth once it is sufficiently known.
(*World Day of Peace Message*, 1991, n. 1)

81. Hence, although the truth we have to proclaim is certain and the salvation necessary, we dare not entertain any thoughts of external coercion. Instead we will use the legitimate means of human friendliness, interior persuasion, and ordinary conversation. We will

offer the gift of salvation while respecting the personal and civic rights of the individual.
(*Ecclesiam Suam,* n. 75)

82. In the first place, religious freedom, an essential requirement of the dignity of every person, is a cornerstone of the structure of human rights, and for this reason an irreplaceable factor in the good of individuals and of the whole society, as well as the personal fulfillment of each individual. It follows that the freedom of individuals and communities to profess and practice their religion is an essential element for peaceful human coexistence. Peace, which is built up and consolidated at all levels of human association, puts down its roots in the freedom and openness of conscience to truth.
(*World Day of Peace Message*, 1988, Introduction)

83. The human issues most frequently debated and differently resolved in contemporary moral reflection are all closely related, albeit in various ways, to a crucial issue: *human freedom.*

Certainly, people today have a particularly strong sense of freedom. As the Council's Declaration on Religious Freedom *Dignitatis Humanae* had already observed, "the dignity of the human person is a concern of which people of our time are becoming increasingly more aware" (*Dignitatis Humanae*, n. 1). Hence, the insistent demand that people be permitted to "enjoy the use of their own responsible judgment and freedom, and decide on their actions on grounds of duty and conscience, without external pressure or coercion" (*Dignitatis Humanae*, n. 1). In particular, the right to religious freedom and to respect for conscience on its journey towards the truth is increasingly perceived as the foundation of the cumulative rights of the person (cf. *Redemptor Hominis*, n. 17; *Libertatis Conscientia*, n. 19).
(*Veritatis Splendor,* n. 31)

ARTICLE THREE

THE FAMILY

I. THE INSTITUTION OF THE FAMILY

84. "Since the Creator of all things has established the conjugal partnership as the beginning and basis of human society," the family is "the first and vital cell of society" (*Apostolicam Actuositatem*, n. 11). The family has vital and organic links with society, since it is its foundation and nourishes it continually through its role of service to life: it is from the family that citizens come to birth, and it is within the family that they find the first school of the social virtues that are the animating principle of the existence and development of society. Thus, far from being closed in on itself, the family is by nature and vocation open to other families and to society, and undertakes its social role.
(*Familiaris Consortio*, n. 42)

85. The first and fundamental structure for 'human ecology' is the family, in which man receives his first formative ideas about truth and goodness, and learns what it means to love and to be loved, and thus what it actually means to be a person. Here we mean the family founded on marriage, in which the mutual gift of self by husband and wife creates an environment in which children can be born and develop their potentialities, become aware of their dignity, and prepare to face their unique and individual destiny. But it often happens that people are discouraged from creating the proper conditions for human reproduction and are led to consider themselves and their lives as a series of sensations to be experienced rather than as a work to be accomplished. The result is a lack of freedom, which causes a person to reject a commitment to enter into a stable relationship with another person and to bring children into the world, or which leads people to consider children as one of the many 'things' that an individual can have or not have, according to taste, and which compete with other possibilities. It is necessary to go back to seeing the

family as the sanctuary of life. The family is indeed sacred: it is the place in which life—the gift of God—can be properly welcomed and protected against the many attacks to which it is exposed, and can develop in accordance with what constitutes authentic human growth. In the face of the so-called culture of death, the family is the heart of the culture of life....
(*Centesimus Annus,* n. 39)

86. But man finds his true identity only in his social milieu, where the family plays a fundamental role. The family's influence may have been excessive, at some periods of history and in some places, when it was exercised to the detriment of the fundamental rights of the individual. The long-standing social frameworks, often too rigid and badly organized, existing in developing countries, are, nevertheless, still necessary for a time, yet progressively relaxing their excessive hold on the population. But the natural family, monogamous and stable, such as the divine plan conceived it and as Christianity sanctified it, must remain the place where "the various generations come together and help one another to grow wiser and to harmonize personal rights with the other requirements of social life" (GS, nn. 50–51).
(*Populorum Progressio*, n. 36)

87. Within the people of life and the people for life, the family has a decisive responsibility. This responsibility flows from its very nature as a community of life and love, founded upon marriage, and from its mission to guard, reveal, and communicate love (*Familiaris Consortio*, n. 17). Here it is a matter of God's love, of which parents are co-workers and, as it were, interpreters when they transmit life and raise it accordingly to his fatherly plan (cf. GS, n. 50).
(*Evangelium Vitae*, n. 92)

88. As the fundamental nucleus of society, the family has a right to the full support of the State in order to carry out fully its particular mission. State laws, therefore, must be directed to promoting its well-being, helping it to fulfill its proper duties. In the face of increasing pressure nowadays to consider, as legally equivalent to the union of spouses, forms of union which by their very nature or their intentional lack of permanence are in no way capable of expressing the meaning and ensuring the good of the family, it is the duty of the State to encourage and protect the authentic institution of the family, respecting its natural structure and its innate and inalienable rights. (*World Day of Peace Message*, 1994, n. 5)

II. MARRIAGE

89. According to the plan of God, marriage is the foundation of the wider community of the family, since the very institution of marriage and conjugal love are ordained to the procreation and education of children, in whom they find their crowning (cf. GS, n. 50). (*Familiaris Consortio*, n. 14)

90. Sexuality is ordered to the conjugal love of man and woman. In marriage, the physical intimacy of the spouses becomes a sign and pledge of spiritual communion. Marriage bonds between baptized persons are sanctified by the sacrament.

"Sexuality, by means of which man and woman give themselves to one another through the acts which are proper and exclusive to spouses, is not something simply biological, but concerns the innermost being of the human person as such. It is realized in a truly human way only if it is an integral part of the love by which a man and woman commit themselves totally to one another until death...."

"The acts in marriage by which the intimate and chaste union of the spouses takes place are noble and honorable; the truly human performance of these acts fosters the self-giving they signify and enriches the spouses in joy and gratitude" (GS, n. 49). Sexuality is a source of joy and pleasure: "The Creator himself ... established that in the (generative) function, spouses should experience pleasure and enjoyment of body and spirit. Therefore, the spouses do nothing evil in seeking this pleasure and enjoyment. They accept what the Creator has intended for them. At the same time, spouses should know how to keep themselves within the limits of just moderation" (Pius XII, Discourse, 1951).

The spouses' union achieves the twofold end of marriage: the good of the spouses themselves and the transmission of life. These two meanings or values of marriage cannot be separated without altering the couple's spiritual life and compromising the goods of marriage and the future of the family.

The conjugal love of man and woman thus stands under the twofold obligation of fidelity and fecundity.
(CCC, nn. 2360–2363)

91. The intimate partnership of married life and love has been established by the Creator and qualified by His laws, and is rooted in the conjugal covenant of irrevocable personal consent. Hence, by that human act whereby spouses mutually bestow and accept each other, a relationship arises which, by divine will and in the eyes of society too, is a lasting one. For the good of the spouses and their offspring's as well as of society, the existence of the sacred bond no longer depends on human decisions alone. For God Himself is the author of matrimony, endowed as it is with various benefits and purposes. All of these have a very decisive bearing on the continuation of the human race, on the personal development and eternal destiny of the individual members of a family, and on the dignity, stability,

peace and prosperity of the family itself and of human society as a whole. By their very nature, the institution of matrimony itself and conjugal love are ordained for the procreation and education of children, and find in them their ultimate crown. Thus a man and a woman, who by their compact of conjugal love "are no longer two, but one flesh" (Mt 19:3ff.), render mutual help and service to each other through an intimate union of their persons and of their actions. Through this union they experience the meaning of their oneness and attain to it with growing perfection day by day. As a mutual gift of two persons, this intimate union and the good of the children impose total fidelity on the spouses and argue for an unbreakable oneness between them.
(*Gaudium et Spes*, n. 48)

92. A certain sharing by man in God's lordship is also evident in the specific responsibility that he is given for human life as such. It is a responsibility that reaches its highest point in the giving of life through procreation by man and woman in marriage. As the Second Vatican Council teaches: "God himself, who said, 'It is not good for man to be alone' (Gn 2:18) and 'who made man from the beginning male and female' (Mt 19:4), wished to share with man a certain special participation in his own creative work. Thus he blessed male and female saying: 'Increase and multiply' (Gn 1:28)" (GS, n. 50). By speaking of "a certain special participation" of man and woman in the "creative work" of God, the Council wishes to point out that having a child is an event which is deeply human and full of religious meaning, insofar as it involves both the spouses, who form "one flesh" (Gn 2:24), and God, who makes himself present.
(*Evangelium Vitae*, n. 43)

III. CHILDREN AND PARENTS

93. When a new person is born of the conjugal union of the two, he brings with him into the world a particular image and likeness of God himself: *the genealogy of the person is inscribed in the very biology of generation.* In affirming that the spouses, as parents, co-operate with God the Creator in conceiving and giving birth to a new human being, we are not speaking merely with reference to the laws of biology. Instead, we wish to emphasize that God *himself is present in human fatherhood and motherhood* quite differently than he is present in all other instances of begetting 'on earth.' Indeed, God alone is the source of that 'image and likeness' which is proper to the human being, as it was received at Creation. Begetting is the continuation of Creation.
(*Gratissimam Sane*, n. 43)

94. In revealing and in reliving on earth the very fatherhood of God (cf. Eph 3:15), a man is called upon to ensure the harmonious and united development of all the members of the family: he will perform this task by exercising generous responsibility for the life conceived under the heart of the mother, by a more solicitous commitment to education, a task he shares with his wife (cf. GS, n. 52), by work, which is never a cause of division in the family but promotes its unity and stability, and by means of the witness he gives of an adult Christian life which effectively introduces the children into the living experience of Christ and the Church.
(*Familiaris Consortio*, n. 25)

95. There is no doubt that the equal dignity and responsibility of men and women fully justifies women's access to public functions. On the other hand, the true advancement of women requires that clear recognition be given to the value of their maternal and

family role, by comparison with all other public roles and all other professions. Furthermore, these roles and professions should be harmoniously combined, if we wish the evolution of society and culture to be truly and fully human.

(Familiaris Consortio, n. 23)

IV. THE FAMILY, EDUCATION, AND CULTURE

96. The task of giving education is rooted in the primary vocation of married couples to participate in God's creative activity: by begetting in love and for love a new person who has within himself or herself the vocation to growth and development, parents by that very fact take on the task of helping that person effectively to live a fully human life. As the Second Vatican Council recalled, "since parents have conferred life on their children, they have a most solemn obligation to educate their offspring. Hence, parents must be acknowledged as the first and foremost educators of their children. Their role as educators is so decisive that scarcely anything can compensate for their failure in it. For it devolves on parents to create a family atmosphere so animated with love and reverence for God and others that a well-rounded personal and social development will be fostered among the children. Hence, the family is the first school of those social virtues that every society needs" (*Gravissimum Educationis*, n. 3). The right and duty of parents to give education is essential, since it is connected with the transmission of human life; it is original and primary with regard to the educational role of others, on account of the uniqueness of the loving relationship between parents and children; and it is irreplaceable and inalienable, and therefore incapable of being entirely delegated to others or usurped by others.

(Familiaris Consortio, n. 36)

97. As already noted, the family, like the State, is by the same token a society in the strictest sense of the term, and is governed by its own proper authority, namely, by that of the father. Wherefore, assuming, of course, that those limits be observed which are fixed by its immediate purpose, the family assuredly possesses rights, at least equal with those of civil society, in respect to choosing and employing the things necessary for its protection and its just liberty. We say "at least equal" because, inasmuch as domestic living together is prior both in thought and in fact to uniting into a polity, it follows that its rights and duties are also prior and more in conformity with nature. But if citizens, if families, after becoming participants in common life and society, were to experience injury in a commonwealth instead of help, impairment of their rights instead of protection, society would be something to be repudiated rather than to be sought for. (*Rerum Novarum*, n. 13)

98. The social role of the family certainly cannot stop short at procreation and education, even if this constitutes its primary and irreplaceable form of expression. Families, therefore, either singly or in association, can and should devote themselves to manifold social service activities, especially in favor of the poor, or, at any rate, for the benefit of all people and situations that cannot be reached by the public authorities' welfare organization. The social contribution of the family has an original character of its own, one that should be given greater recognition and more decisive encouragement, especially as the children grow up, and actually involving all its members as much as possible.
(*Familiaris Consortio*, n. 44)

99. To desire, therefore, that the civil power should enter arbitrarily into the privacy of homes is a great and pernicious error. If a family perchance is in such extreme difficulty and is so completely

without plans that it is entirely unable to help itself, it is right that the distress be remedied by public aid, for each individual family is a part of the community. Similarly, if anywhere there is a grave violation of mutual rights within the family walls, public authority shall restore to each his right; for this is not usurping the rights of citizens, but protecting and confirming them with just and due care. Those in charge of public affairs, however, must stop here; nature does not permit them to go beyond these limits.
(*Rerum Novarum*, n. 14)

100. Within the "people of life and the people for life," *the family has a decisive responsibility.* This responsibility flows from its very nature as a community of life and love, founded upon marriage, and from its mission to "guard, reveal and communicate love" (*Familiaris Consortio*, n. 17). Here it is a matter of God's own love, of which parents are co-workers and, as it were, interpreters when they transmit life and raise it according to his fatherly plan (cf. GS, n. 50). This is the love that becomes selflessness, receptiveness and gift. Within the family each member is accepted, respected and honored precisely because he or she is a person; and if any family member is in greater need, the care which he or she receives is all the more intense and attentive.

The family has a special role to play throughout the life of its members, from birth to death. It is truly "the *sanctuary of life*: the place in which life—the gift of God—can be properly welcomed and protected against the many attacks to which it is exposed, and can develop in accordance with what constitutes authentic human growth" (CA, n. 39). Consequently, the role of the family in building a culture of life is *decisive and irreplaceable.*

As the *domestic church,* the family is summoned to proclaim, celebrate and serve the *Gospel of life.* This is a responsibility which first concerns married couples, called to be givers of life, on the

basis of an ever greater *awareness of the meaning of procreation* as a unique event which clearly reveals that *human life is a gift received in order then to be given as a gift.* In giving origin to a new life, parents recognize that the child, "as the fruit of their mutual gift of love, is, in turn, a gift for both of them, a gift which flows from them" (John Paul II, *Address to the Seventh Symposium of European Bishops*, 1989, n. 5).
(*Evangelium Vitae,* n. 92)

101. The Gospel of life is at the heart of Jesus' message. Lovingly received day after day by the Church, it is to be preached with dauntless fidelity as "good news" to the people of every age and culture.

At the dawn of salvation, it is the Birth of a Child which is proclaimed as joyful news: "I bring you good news of a great joy which will come to all the people; for to you is born this day in the city of David a Savior, who is Christ the Lord" (Lk 2:10–11). The source of this "great joy" is the Birth of the Savior; but Christmas also reveals the full meaning of every human birth, and the joy which accompanies the Birth of the Messiah is thus seen to be the foundation and fulfillment of joy at every child born into the world (cf. Jn 16:21).

When he presents the heart of his redemptive mission, Jesus says: "I came that they may have life, and have it abundantly" (Jn 10:10). In truth, he is referring to that "new" and "eternal" life which consists in communion with the Father, to which every person is freely called in the Son by the power of the Sanctifying Spirit. It is precisely in this "life" that all the aspects and stages of human life achieve their full significance.
(*Evangelium Vitae,* n. 1)

V. THE SANCTITY OF HUMAN LIFE

102. Man's life comes from God; it is his gift, his image and imprint, a sharing in his breath of life. God, therefore, is the sole Lord of this life: man cannot do with it as he wills. God himself makes this clear to Noah after the flood: "For your own lifeblood, too, I will demand an accounting ... and from man in regard to his fellow man I will demand an accounting of human life" (Gn 9:5). The biblical text is concerned to emphasize how the sacredness of life has its foundation in God and in his creative activity: "For God made man in his own image" (Gn 9:6).
(*Evangelium Vitae*, n. 39)

103. "Human life is sacred because from its beginning it involves the 'creative action of God' and it remains forever in a special relationship with the Creator, who is its sole end. God alone is the Lord of life from its beginning until its end: no one can, in any circumstance, claim for himself the right to destroy directly an innocent human being." With these words, *Donum Vitae* (DV, n. 7) sets forth the central content of God's revelation on the sacredness and inviolability of human life.
(*Evangelium Vitae*, n. 53)

104. The inviolability of the person, which is a reflection of the absolute inviolability of God, finds its primary and fundamental expression in the 'inviolability of human life.' Above all, the common outcry, which is justly made on behalf of human rights—for example, the right to health, to home, to work, to family, to culture—is false and illusory if 'the right to life,' the most basic and fundamental right and the condition for all other personal rights, is not defended with maximum determination. The Church has never yielded in the face of all the violations that the right to life of every human being has

51

received, and continues to receive, both from individuals and from those in authority. The human being is entitled to such rights, 'in every phase of development,' from conception until natural death; and in 'every condition,' whether healthy or sick, whole or handicapped, rich or poor.
(*Christifideles Laici*, n. 38)

105. The Church today lives a fundamental aspect of her mission in lovingly and generously accepting every human being, especially those who are weak and sick. This is made all the more necessary as a 'culture of death' threatens to take control. In fact, "the Church family believes that human life, even if weak and suffering, is always a wonderful gift of God's goodness. Against the pessimism and selfishness which casts a shadow over the world, the Church stands for life: in each human life she sees the splendour of that 'Yes,' that 'Amen,' which is Christ himself (cf. 2 Cor 1:19; Rv 3:14). To the 'No' which assails and afflicts the world, she replies with this living 'Yes,' this defending of the human person and the world from all who plot against life" (*Familiaris Consortio*, n. 30). It is the responsibility of the lay faithful, who more directly through their vocation or their profession are involved in accepting life, to make the Church's 'Yes' to human life concrete and efficacious.
(*Christifideles Laici*, n. 38)

106. Reason attests that there are objects of the human act which are by their nature "incapable of being ordered" to God, because they radically contradict the good of the person made in his image. These are the acts which, in the Church's moral tradition, have been termed 'intrinsically evil' (*intrinsece malum*): they are such *always and per se,* in other words, on account of their very object, and quite apart from the ulterior intentions of the one acting and the circumstances. Consequently, without in the least denying the influence on

morality exercised by circumstances and especially by intentions, the Church teaches that "there exist acts which *per se* and in themselves, independently of circumstances, are always seriously wrong by reason of their object" (*Reconciliato et Paenitentia, n.* 17). The Second Vatican Council itself, in discussing the respect due to the human person, gives a number of examples of such acts: "Whatever is hostile to life itself, such as any kind of homicide, genocide, abortion, euthanasia and voluntary suicide; whatever violates the integrity of the human person, such as mutilation, physical and mental torture and attempts to coerce the spirit; whatever is offensive to human dignity, such as subhuman living conditions, arbitrary imprisonment, deportation, slavery, prostitution and trafficking in women and children; degrading conditions of work which treat laborers as mere instruments of profit, and not as free responsible persons: all these and the like are a disgrace, and so long as they infect human civilization, they contaminate those who inflict them more than those who suffer injustice, and they are a negation of the honor due to the Creator" (GS, n. 27). (*Veritatis Splendor,* n. 80)

VI. The Evil of Abortion and Euthanasia

107. Human life finds itself most vulnerable when it enters the world and when it leaves the realm of time to embark upon eternity. The word of God frequently repeats the call to show care and respect, above all where life is undermined by sickness and old age. Although there are no direct and explicit calls to protect human life at its very beginning, specifically life not yet born, and life nearing its end, this can be easily explained by the fact that the mere possibility of harming, attacking, or actually denying life in these circumstances is completely foreign to the religious and cultural way of thinking of the People of God.

(Evangelium Vitae, n. 44)

108. Nothing and no one can in any way permit the killing of an innocent human being, whether fetus or an embryo, an infant or an adult, an old person, or one suffering from an incurable disease, or a person who is dying. Furthermore, no one is permitted to ask for this act of killing, either for himself or herself or for another person entrusted to his or her care, nor can he or she consent to it, either explicitly or implicitly. Nor can any authority legitimately recommend or permit such an action.
(Iura et Bona, n. 2)

109. Therefore, by the authority which Christ conferred on Peter and to his Successors, and in communion with the Bishops of the Catholic Church, I confirm that the direct and voluntary killing of an innocent human being is always gravely immoral. This doctrine, based upon the unwritten law which man, in the light of reason, finds in his own heart (cf. Rom 2:14–15), is reaffirmed by the Sacred Scripture, transmitted by the Tradition of the Church and taught by the ordinary and universal Magisterium.
(Evangelium Vitae, n. 57)

110. I would now like to say a special word to *women who have had an abortion.* The Church is aware of the many factors which may have influenced your decision, and she does not doubt that in many cases it was a painful and even shattering decision. The wound in your heart may not yet have healed. Certainly what happened was and remains terribly wrong. But do not give in to discouragement and do not lose hope. Try rather to understand what happened and face it honestly. If you have not already done so, give yourselves over with humility and trust to repentance. The Father of mercies is ready to give you his forgiveness and his peace in the Sacrament of

Reconciliation. You will come to understand that nothing is definitively lost, and you will also be able to ask forgiveness from your child, who is now living in the Lord. With the friendly and expert help and advice of other people, and as a result of your own painful experience, you can be among the most eloquent defenders of everyone's right to life. Through your commitment to life, whether by accepting the birth of other children or by welcoming and caring for those most in need of someone to be close to them, you will become promoters of a new way of looking at human life. (*Evangelium Vitae*, n. 99)

VII. CAPITAL PUNISHMENT

111. "Legitimate defense can be not only a right but a grave duty for another's life. Preserving the common good requires rendering the unjust aggressor unable to inflict harm. To this end, those holding legitimate authority have the right to repel by armed force aggressors against the civil community entrusted to their charge" (Aquinas, *STh*, II-II, 64, 7). The State's effort to contain the spread of behaviors injurious to human rights and the fundamental rules of civil coexistence corresponds to the requirement of watching over the common good. Legitimate public authority has the right and duty to inflict penalities commensurate with the gravity of the crime. The primary scope of the penalty is to redress the disorder caused by the offense. When this punishment is voluntarily accepted by the offender, it takes on the value of expiation. Moreover, punishment, in addition to preserving public order and the safety of persons, has a medicinal scope: as far as possible it should contribute to the correction of the offender (cf. Lk 23:40–43).
(CCC, nn. 2265–2266)

112. [T]here is a growing tendency, both in the Church and in

civil society, to demand that [the death penalty] be applied in a very limited way or even that it be abolished completely. The problem must be viewed in the context of a system of penal justice ever more in line with human dignity and thus, in the end, with God's plan for man and society. The primary purpose of punishment which society inflicts is "to redress the disorder caused by the offense" (CCC, n. 2266). Public authority must redress the violation of personal and social rights by imposing on the offender an adequate punishment for the crime, as a condition for the offender to regain the exercise of his or her freedom. In this way authority also fulfills the purpose of defending public order and ensuring people's safety, while ... offering the offender an incentive and help to change his or her behavior and be rehabilitated (CCC, n. 2266).

It is clear that, for these purposes to be achieved, *the nature and extent of the punishment* must be carefully evaluated and decided upon, and ought not go to the extreme of executing the offender except in cases of absolute necessity: in other words, when it would not be possible otherwise to defend society. Today, however, as a result of steady improvements in the organization of the penal system, such cases are very rare, if not practically non-existent.
(*Evangelium Vitae*, n. 56)

113. The traditional teaching of the Church does not exclude, presupposing full ascertainment of the identity and responsibility of the offender, recourse to the death penalty, when this is the only practicable way to defend the lives of human beings effectively against the aggressor. If, instead, bloodless means are sufficient to defend against the aggressor and to protect the safety of persons, public authority should limit itself to such means, because they better correspond to the concrete conditions of the common good and are in conformity to the dignity of the human person. Today, in fact, given the means at the State's disposal to effectively repress crime by ren-

dering inoffensive the one who has committed it, without depriving him definitively of the possibility of redeeming himself, cases of absolute necessity for suppression of the offender "today ... are very rare, if not practically non-existent" (*Evangelium Vitae*, n. 56). (CCC, n. 2267)

VIII. THE DIGNITY OF WOMEN

114. Certainly much remains to be done to prevent discrimination against those who have chosen to be wives and mothers. As far as personal rights are concerned, there is an urgent need to achieve real equality in every area: equal pay for equal work, protection for working mothers, fairness in career advancements, equality of spouses with regard to family rights, and the recognition of everything that is part of the rights and duties of citizens of a democratic state. This is a matter of justice but also of necessity. Women will increasingly play a part in the solution of the serious problems of the future: leisure time, the quality of life, migration, social services, euthanasia, drugs, health care, the ecology, etc. In all these areas a greater presence of women in society will prove most valuable, for it will help to manifest the contradictions present when society is organized solely according to the criteria of efficiency and productivity, and it will force systems to be redesigned in a way which favors the processes of humanization which mark the "civilization of love."
(*Letter to Women*, n. 4)

115. Part of this daily heroism is also the silent but effective and eloquent witness of all those "brave mothers who devote themselves to their own family without reserve, who suffer in giving birth to their children and who are ready to make any effort, to face any sacrifice, in order to pass on to them the best of themselves" (John

Paul II, Homily for Beatification, 1994). In living out their mission, "these heroic women do not always find support in the world around them. On the contrary, the cultural models frequently promoted and broadcast by the media do not encourage motherhood. In the name of progress and modernity the values of fidelity, chastity, sacrifice, to which a host of Christian wives and mothers have borne and continue to bear outstanding witness, are presented as obsolete.... We thank you, heroic mothers, for your invincible love! We thank you for your intrepid trust in God and in his love. We thank you for the sacrifice of your life.... In the Paschal Mystery, Christ restores to you the gift you gave him. Indeed, he has the power to give you back the life you gave him as an offering" (John Paul II, Homily for Beatification, 1994).
(*Evangelium Vitae,* n. 86)

116. "God created man in his own image, in the image of God he created him; male and female he created them" (Gn 1:27). This concise passage contains the fundamental anthropological truths: man is the high point of the whole order of creation in the visible world; the human race, which takes its origin from the calling into existence of man and woman, crowns the whole work of creation; both man and woman are human beings to an equal degree; both are created in God's image. This image and likeness of God, which is essential for the human being, is passed on by the woman and the man, as spouses and parents, to their descendents: "Be fruitful and multiply, and fill the earth and subdue it" (Gn 1:28). The creator entrusts dominion over the earth to the human race, to all persons, to all men and women, who derive their dignity and vocation from the common beginning.
(*Mulieris Dignitatem,* n. 4)

117. In transforming culture so that it supports life, *women* oc-

cupy a place, in thought and action, which is unique and decisive. It depends on them to promote a 'new feminism' which rejects the temptation of imitating models of 'male domination,' in order to acknowledge and affirm the true genius of women in every aspect of the life of society, and overcome all discrimination, violence and exploitation. Making my own the words of the concluding message of the Second Vatican Council, I address to women this urgent appeal: *"Reconcile people with life"* (*Closing Message of The Council* [1965]: *To Women*). You are called to *bear witness to the meaning of genuine love,* of that gift of self and of that acceptance of others which are present in a special way in the relationship of husband and wife, but which ought also to be at the heart of every other interpersonal relationship.... "Motherhood involves a special communion with the mystery of life, as it develops in the woman's womb.... This unique contact with the new human being developing within her gives rise to an attitude towards human beings not only towards her own child, but every human being, which profoundly marks the woman's personality" (*Mulieris Dignitatem*, n. 18). A mother welcomes and carries in herself another human being, enabling it to grow inside her, giving it room, respecting it in its otherness. Women first learn and then teach others that human relations are authentic if they are open to accepting the other person: a person who is recognized and loved because of the dignity which comes from being a person and not from other considerations, such as usefulness, strength, intelligence, beauty or health. This is the fundamental contribution which the Church and humanity expect from women. And it is the indispensable prerequisite for an authentic cultural change.
(*Evangelium Vitae,* n. 99)

ARTICLE FOUR

THE SOCIAL ORDER

I. THE CENTRALITY OF THE HUMAN PERSON

118. The cardinal point of this teaching is that individual men are necessarily the foundation, cause, and end of all social institutions. We are referring to human beings, insofar as they are social by nature, and raised to an order of existence that transcends and subdues nature.
(*Mater et Magistra*, n. 219)

119. In the economic and social realms, too, the dignity and complete vocation of the human person and the welfare of society as a whole are to be respected and promoted. For man is the source, the center, and the purpose of all economic and social life.
(*Gaudium et Spes,* n. 63)

120. Man, in keeping with the openness of his spirit within and also with the many diverse needs of his body and his existence in time, writes this personal history of his through numerous bonds, contacts, situations, and social structures linking him with other men, beginning to do so from the first moment of his existence on earth, from the moment of his conception and birth. Man, in the full truth of his existence, of his personal being and also his community and social being, in the sphere of his own family, in the sphere of society and very diverse contexts, in the sphere of his own nation or people (perhaps still only that of his clan or his tribe), and in the sphere of the whole of mankind—this man is the primary route the Church must travel in fulfilling her mission: he is the primary and fundamental way for the Church, the way traced out by Christ himself, the way that leads invariably through the mystery of the Incarnation and the Redemption.
(*Redemptor Hominis*, n. 14)

121. The foundation and goal of the social order is the human person, as a subject of inalienable rights which are not conferred from the outside but which arise from the person's very nature.... Likewise, the person is not merely the subject of social, cultural, and historical conditioning, for it is proper to man, who has a spiritual soul, to tend towards a goal that transcends the changing conditions of his existence. No human power may obstruct the realization of man as a person.
(*World Day of Peace Message*, 1988, n. 1)

II. SOCIETY FOUNDED ON TRUTH

122. A civic society is to be considered well-ordered, beneficial and in keeping with human dignity if it is grounded on truth. As the Apostle Paul exhorts us: "Away with falsehood then; let everyone speak out the truth to his neighbor; membership of the body binds us to one another" (Eph 4:25). This will be accomplished when each one duly recognizes both his rights and his obligations towards others.
(*Pacem in Terris*, n. 35)

123. The Supreme good and the moral good meet in truth: the truth of God, the Creator and Redeemer, and the truth of man, created and redeemed by him. Only upon this truth is it possible to construct a renewed society and to solve the complex and weighty problems affecting it, above all, the problem of overcoming the various forms of totalitarianism, so as to make way for the authentic freedom of the person. "Totalitarianism arises out of a denial of truth in the objective sense. If there is no transcendent truth, in obedience to which man achieves his full identity, then there is no sure principle for guaranteeing just relations between people. Their self-interest

as a class, group or nation would inevitably set them in opposition to one another" (CA, n. 44).
(*Veritatis Splendor*, n. 99)

124. First among the rules governing the relations between States is that of truth. This calls, above all, for the elimination of every trace of racism, and the consequent recognition of the principle that all States are by nature equal in dignity. Each of them accordingly is vested with the right to existence, to self-development, to the means fitting to its attainment, and to be the one primarily responsible for this self-development. Add to that the right of each to its good name, and to the respect which is its due.
(*Pacem in Terris*, n. 86)

125. In the light of faith, solidarity seeks to go beyond itself, to take on the specifically Christian dimension of total gratuity, forgiveness and reconciliation. One's neighbor is then not only a human being with his or her own rights and a fundamental equality with everyone else, but becomes the living image of God the Father, redeemed by the blood of Jesus Christ and placed under the permanent action of the Holy Spirit. One's neighbor must therefore be loved, even if an enemy, with the same love with which the Lord loves him or her; and for that person's sake one must be ready for sacrifice, even the ultimate one: to lay down one's life for the brethren (cf. 1 Jn 3:16).

At that point, awareness of the common fatherhood of God, of the brotherhood of all in Christ—'children in the Son'—and of the presence and life-giving action of the Holy Spirit will bring to our vision of the world a new criterion for interpreting it. Beyond human and natural bonds, already so close and strong, there is discerned in the light of faith a new model of the unity of the human race, which must ultimately inspire our solidarity. This supreme model of unity, which is a reflection of the intimate life of God, one God in three

Persons, is what we Christians mean by the word 'communion.' This specifically Christian communion, jealously preserved, extended and enriched with the Lord's help, is the soul of the Church's vocation to be a 'sacrament,' in the sense already indicated.
(*Sollicitudo Rei Socialis*, n. 40)

III. SOLIDARITY

126. [Solidarity], then, is not a feeling of vague compassion or shallow distress at the misfortunes of so many people, both near and far. On the contrary, it is a firm and persevering determination to commit oneself to the common good; that is to say, to the good of all and of each individual, because we are all really responsible for all. This determination is based on the solid conviction that what is hindering full development is that desire for profit and that thirst for power already mentioned. These attitudes and 'structures of sin' are only conquered—presupposing the help of divine grace—by a diametrically opposed attitude: a commitment to the good of one's neighbor with the readiness, in the gospel sense, to 'lose oneself' for the sake of the other instead of exploiting him, and to 'serve him' instead of oppressing him for one's own advantage (cf. Mt 10:40–42; 20:25; Mk 10:42–45; Lk 22:25–27).
(*Sollicitudo Rei Socialis*, n. 38)

127. In the spirit of solidarity and with the instruments of dialogue we will learn: respect for every human person; respect for the true values and cultures of others; respect for the legitmate autonomy and self-determination of others; to look beyond ourselves in order to understand and support the good of others; to contribute to our own resources in social solidarity for the development and growth that come from equity and justice; to build structures that will ensure

that social solidarity and dialogue are permanent features of the world we live in.
(*World Day of Peace Message*, 1986, n. 5)

128. The same duty of solidarity that rests on individuals exists also for nations: "Advanced nations have a very heavy obligation to help the developing peoples" (GS, n. 86). It is necessary to put this teaching of the Council into effect. Although it is normal that a nation should be the first to benefit from the gifts that Providence has bestowed on it as the fruit of the labors of its people, still no country can claim on that account to keep its wealth for itself alone. Every nation must produce more and better quality goods to give to all its inhabitants a truly human standard of living, and also to contribute to the common development of the human race. Given the increasing needs of the under-developed countries, it should be considered quite normal for an advanced country to devote a part of its production to meet their needs, and to train teachers, engineers, technicians and scholars prepared to put their knowledge and their skill at the disposal of less fortunate peoples.
(*Populorum Progressio*, n. 48)

129. In order to overcome today's widespread individualistic mentality, what is required is a concrete commitment to solidarity and charity, beginning in the family with the mutual support of husband and wife and the care which the different generations give to one another. In this sense the family, too, can be called a community of work and solidarity.
(*Centesimus Annus*, n. 49)

130. We are all united in this progress toward God. We have desired to remind all men how crucial is the present moment, how urgent the work to be done. The hour for action has now sounded. At

stake are the survival of so many innocent children and, for so many families overcome by misery, the access to conditions fit for human beings; at stake are the peace of the world and the future of civilization. It is time for all men and all peoples to face up to their responsibilities.
(*Populorum Progressio*, n. 80)

131. The exercise of solidarity within each society is valid when its members recognize one another as persons. Those who are more influential, because they have a greater share of goods and common services, should feel responsible for the weaker and be ready to share with them all they possess. Those who are weaker, for their part, in the same spirit of solidarity, should not adopt a purely passive attitude or one that is destructive of the social fabric, but, while claiming their legitimate rights, should do what they can for the good of all. The intermediate groups, in their turn, should not selfishly insist on their particular interests, but respect the interests of others.
(*Sollicitudo Rei Socialis*, n. 39)

132. In this way what we nowadays call the principle of solidarity, the validity of which both in the internal order of each nation and in the international order I have discussed in the Encyclical *Sollicitudo Rei Socialis* (cf. SRS, nn. 38–40), is clearly seen to be one of the fundamental principles of the Christian view of social and political organization. This principle is frequently stated by Pope Leo XIII, who uses the term 'friendship,' a concept already found in Greek philosophy. Pope Pius XI refers to it with the equally meaningful term 'social charity.' Pope Paul VI, expanding the concept to cover the many modern aspects of the social question, speaks of a 'civilization of love' (cf. RN, n. 25; QA, n. 3; Paul VI, Homily for the Closing of the Holy Year, 1975).
(*Centesimus Annus*, n. 10)

133. Solidarity helps us to see the 'other'—whether a person, people or nation—not just as some kind of instrument, with a work capacity and physical strength to be exploited at low cost and then discarded when no longer useful, but as our 'neighbor,' a 'helper' (cf. Gn 2:18–20) to be made a sharer, on a par with ourselves, in the banquet of life to which all are equally invited by God. (*Sollicitudo Rei Socialis*, n. 39)

IV. SUBSIDIARITY

134. The teaching of the Church has elaborated the principle of subsidiarity, according to which "a community of a higher order should not interfere in the internal life of a community of a lower order, depriving the latter of its functions, but rather should support it in case of need and help to co-ordinate its activity with the activities of the rest of society, always with a view to the common good" (CA, n. 48; cf. QA, nn. 184–186). God has not willed to reserve to himself all exercise of power. He entrusts to every creature the functions it is capable of performing, according to the capacities of its own nature. This mode of governance ought to be followed in social life. The way God acts in governing the world, which bears witness to such great regard for human freedom, should inspire the wisdom of those who govern human communities. They should behave as ministers of divine providence. The principle of subsidiarity is opposed to all forms of collectivism. It sets limits for state intervention. It aims at harmonizing the relationships between individuals and societies. It tends toward the establishment of true international order. (CCC, nn. 1883–1885)

135. Moreover, just as it is necessary in each state that relations which the public authority has with its citizens, families and

intermediate associations be controlled and regulated by the principle of subsidiarity, it is equally necessary that the relationships which exist between the worldwide public authority and the public authorities of individual nations be governed by the same principle. This means that the worldwide public authority must tackle and solve problems of an economic, social, political or cultural character which are posed by the universal common good. For, because of the vastness, complexity and urgency of those problems, the public authorities of the individual states are not in a position to tackle them with any hope of a positive solution. The worldwide public authority is not intended to limit the sphere of action of the public authority of the individual state, much less to take its place. On the contrary, its purpose is to create, on a world basis, an environment in which the public authorities of each state, its citizens and intermediate associations, can carry out their tasks, fulfill their duties and exercise their rights with greater security.

(*Pacem in Terris*, nn. 140–141)

136. At the outset it should be affirmed that in economic affairs first place is to be given to the private initiative of individual men who, either working by themselves, or with others in one fashion or another, pursue their common interests.

(*Mater et Magistra*, n. 51)

137. Nevertheless, it remains true that precautionary activities of public authorities in the economic field, although widespread and penetrating, should be such that they not only avoid restricting the freedom of private citizens, but also increase it, so long as the basic rights of each individual person are preserved inviolate. Included among these is the right and duty of each individual normally to provide the necessities of life for himself and his dependents. This implies that whatever be the economic system, it allow and facilitate

for every individual the opportunity to engage in productive activity. (*Mater et Magistra*, n. 55)

138. In this regard, *Rerum Novarum* points the way to just reforms which can restore dignity to work as the free activity of man. These reforms imply that society and the State will both assume responsibility, especially for protecting the worker from the nightmare of unemployment. Historically, this has happened in two converging ways: either through economic policies aimed at ensuring balanced growth and full employment, or through unemployment insurance and retraining programs capable of ensuring a smooth transfer of workers from crisis sectors to those in expansion.... The State must contribute to the achievement of these goals both directly and indirectly. Indirectly and according to the principle of subsidiarity, by creating favorable conditions for the free exercise of economic activity, which will lead to abundant opportunities for employment and sources of wealth. Directly and according to the principle of solidarity, by defending the weakest, by placing certain limits on the autonomy of the parties who determine working conditions, and by ensuring in every case the necessary minimum support for the unemployed worker. (*Centesimus Annus,* n. 15)

V. Participation

139. The two aspirations, to equality and to participation, seek to promote a democratic type of society. Various models are proposed, some are tried out, none of them gives complete satisfaction, and the search goes on between ideological and pragmatic tendencies. The Christian has the duty to take part in this search and in the organization and life of political society. As a social being, man builds

his destiny within a series of particular groupings which demand, as their completion and as a necessary condition for their development, a vaster society, one of a universal character, the political society. All particular activity must be placed within that wider society, and thereby it takes on the dimension of the common good.
(*Octogesima Adveniens*, n. 24)

140. It is essential for every human being to have a sense of participating, of being a part of the decisions and endeavors that shape the destiny of the world. Violence and injustice have often in the past found their root causes in people's sense of being deprived of the right to shape their own lives. Future violence and injustice cannot be avoided when the basic right to participate in the choices of society is denied.
(*World Day of Peace Message*, 1985, n. 9)

141. It is a strict duty of justice and truth not to allow fundamental human needs to remain unsatisfied, and not allow those burdened by such needs to perish. It is also necessary to help these needy people to acquire expertise, to enter the circle of exchange, and to develop their skills in order to make the best use of their capacities and resources.
(*Centesimus Annus*, n. 34)

142. It is in full accord with human nature that juridical–political structures should, with ever better success and without any discrimination, afford all their citizens the chance to participate freely and actively in establishing the constitutional bases of a political community, governing the state, determining the scope and purpose of various institutions, and choosing leaders.... Authorities must beware of hindering family, social, or cultural groups, as well as intermediate bodies and institutions. They must not deprive them of their own

lawful and effective activity, but should rather strive to promote them willingly and in an orderly fashion. For their part, citizens both as individuals and in association should be on guard against granting government too much authority and inappropriately seeking from it excessive conveniences and advantages, with a consequent weakening of the sense of responsibility on the part of individuals, families, and social groups.
(*Gaudium et Spes*, n. 75)

143. All citizens have the right to participate in the life of their community: this is a conviction which is generally shared today. But this right means nothing when the democratic process breaks down because of corruption and favoritism, which not only obstruct legitimate sharing in the exercise of power but also prevent people from benefitting equally from community assets and services, to which everyone has a right.
(*World Day of Peace Message*, 1999, n. 6)

144. While scientific and technological progress continues to overturn man's surrounding, his patterns of knowledge, work, consumption and relationships, two aspirations persistently make themselves felt in these new contexts, and they grow stronger to the extent that he becomes better informed and better educated: the aspiration to equality and the aspiration to participation, two forms of man's dignity and freedom.
(*Octogesima Adveniens*, n. 22)

145. The dignity of the human person involves the right to take an active part in public affairs and to contribute one's part to the common good of the citizens. For, as Our Predecessor of happy memory, Pius XII, pointed out: "The human individual, far from being an object and, as it were, a merely passive element in the social

order, is, in fact, must be and must continue to be, its subject, its foundation and its end" (Christmas Eve Radio Message, 1944). (*Pacem in Terris*, n. 26)

VI. ALIENATION AND MARGINALIZATION

146. Marxism criticized capitalist bourgeois societies, blaming them for the commercialization and alienation of human existence. This rebuke is of course based on a mistaken and inadequate idea of alienation, derived solely from the sphere of relationships of production and ownership, that is, giving them a materialistic foundation and moreover denying the legitimacy and positive value of market relationships even in their own sphere.... [N]evertheless, alienation— and the loss of the authentic meaning of life—is a reality in Western societies too. This happens in consumerism, when people are ensnared in a web of false and superficial gratifications rather than being helped to experience their personhood in an authentic and concrete way. Alienation is found also in work, when it is organized so as to ensure maximum returns and profits with no concern whether the worker, through his own labor, grows or diminishes as a person, either through increased sharing in a genuinely supportive community or through increased isolation in a maze of relationships marked by destructive competitiveness and estrangement, in which he is considered only a means to an end. The concept of alienation needs to be led back to the Christian vision of reality, by recognizing in alienation a reversal of means and ends. When man does not recognize in himself and in others the value and grandeur of the human person, he effectively deprives himself of the possibility of benefiting from his humanity and of entering into that relationship of solidarity and communion with others for which God created him. (*Centesimus Annus*, n. 41)

147. The man of today seems ever to be under threat from what he produces, that is to say from the result of the work of his hands and, even more so, of the work of his intellect and the tendencies of his will. All too soon, and often in an unforeseeable way, what this manifold activity of man yields is not only subjected to alienation, in the sense that it is simply taken away from the person who produces it, but rather it turns against man himself, at least in part through the indirect consequences of its effects returning on himself.
(*Redemptor Hominis*, n. 15)

148. The question of morality, to which Christ provides the answer, cannot prescind from the issue of freedom. Indeed, it considers that issue central, for there can be no morality without freedom: "It is only in freedom that man can turn to what is good" (GS, n. 17). But what sort of freedom? The Council, considering our contemporaries who "highly regard" freedom and "assiduously pursue" it, but who "often cultivate it in wrong ways as a license to do anything they please, even evil," speaks of "genuine" freedom: "Genuine freedom is an outstanding manifestation of the divine image in man. For God willed to leave man 'in the power of his own counsel' (cf. Sir 15:14), so that he would seek his Creator of his own accord and would freely arrive at full and blessed perfection by cleaving to God" (GS, n. 17). Although each individual has a right to be respected in his own journey in search of the truth, there exists a prior moral obligation, and a grave one at that, to seek the truth and to adhere to it once it is known (cf. *Dignitatis Humanae*, n. 2).
(*Veritatis Splendor*, n. 34)

149. Not only is it wrong from the ethical point of view to disregard human nature, which is made for freedom, but in practice it is impossible to do so. Where society is so organized as to reduce arbitrarily or even suppress the sphere in which freedom is legitimately

exercised, the result is that the life of society becomes progressively disorganized and goes into decline.
(*Centesimus Annus*, n. 25)

150. Freedom is the measure of man's dignity and greatness. Living the freedom sought by individuals and peoples is a great challenge to man's spiritual growth and to the moral vitality of nations.
(*Address to the Fiftieth General Assembly of the United Nations Organization,* 1995, n. 12)

151. Freedom is not simply the absence of tyranny or oppression. Nor is freedom a license to do whatever we like. Freedom has an inner 'logic' which distinguishes it and ennobles it: freedom is ordered to the truth, and is fulfilled in man's quest for truth and in man's living in the truth. Detached from the truth about the human person, freedom deteriorates into license in the lives of individuals, and, in political life, it becomes the caprice of the most powerful and the arrogance of power.
(*Address to the Fiftieth General Assembly of the United Nations Organization*, 1995, n. 12)

VII. SOCIAL FREEDOM

152. Since it is not an ideology, the Christian faith does not presume to imprison changing socio-political realities in a rigid schema, and it recognizes that human life is realized in history in conditions that are diverse and imperfect. Furthermore, in constantly reaffirming the transcendent dignity of the person, the Church's method is always that of respect for freedom.
(*Centesimus Annus*, n. 46)

153. It has also to be borne in mind that relations between States should be based on freedom, that is to say, that no country may unjustly oppress others or unduly meddle in their affairs. On the contrary, all should help to develop in others a sense of responsibility, a spirit of enterprise, and an earnest desire to be the first to promote their own advancement in every field.
(*Pacem in Terris*, n. 120)

154. Consequently, the inseparable connection between truth and freedom—which expresses the essential bond between God's wisdom and will—is extremely significant for the life of persons in the socio-economic and socio-political sphere.
(*Veritatis Splendor*, n. 99)

VIII. CULTURE

155. There are many ties between the message of salvation and human culture. For God, revealing Himself to His people to the extent of a full manifestation of Himself in His Incarnate Son, has spoken according to the culture proper to each epoch. Likewise, the Church, living in various circumstances in the course of time, has used the discoveries of different cultures so that in her preaching she might spread and explain the message of Christ to all nations, that she might examine it and more deeply understand it, that she might give it better expression in liturgical celebration and in the varied life of the community of the faithful.

But at the same time, the Church, sent to all peoples of every time and place, is not bound exclusively and indissolubly to any race or nation, any particular way of life or any customary way of life recent or ancient. Faithful to her own tradition and at the same time conscious of her universal mission, she can enter into communion with the various civilizations, to their enrichment and the enrichment of the Church herself.

The Gospel of Christ constantly renews the life and culture of fallen man; it combats and removes the errors and evils resulting from the permanent allurement of sin. It never eases to purify and elevate the morality of peoples. By riches coming from above, it makes fruitful, as it were from within, the spiritual qualities and traditions of every people and of every age. It strengthens, perfects and restores them in Christ. Thus the Church, in the very fulfillment of her own function, stimulates and advances human and civic culture; by her action, also by her liturgy, she leads them toward interior liberty. (*Gaudium et Spes,* n. 58)

156. All human activity takes place within a culture and interacts with culture. For an adequate formation of a culture, the involvement of the whole man is required, whereby he exercises his creativity, intelligence, and knowledge of the world and of people. Furthermore, he displays his capacity for self-control, personal sacrifice, solidarity and readiness to promote the common good. Thus, the first and most important task is accomplished within man's heart. The way in which he is involved in building his own future depends on the understanding he has of himself and of his own destiny. (*Centesimus Annus*, n. 51)

157. Rich or poor, each country possesses a civilization handed down by their ancestors: institutions called for by life in this world, and higher manifestations of the life of the spirit, manifestations of an artistic, intellectual and religious character. When the latter possess true human values, it would be grave error to sacrifice them to the former. A people that would act in this way would thereby lose the best of its patrimony; in order to live, it would be sacrificing its reasons for living. Christ's teaching also applies to people: "What

does it profit a man to gain the whole world if he suffers the loss of his soul?" (Mt 16:26)

(*Populorum Progressio,* n. 40)

158. Culture is the vital space within which the human person comes face to face with the Gospel. Just as culture is the result of life and activity of a human group, so the persons belonging to that group are shaped to a large extent by the culture in which they live. As persons and society change, so too does the culture change with them. As a culture is transformed, so too are persons and societies transformed by it. From this perspective, it becomes clearer why evangelization and inculturation are naturally and intimately related to each other. The Gospel and evangelization are certainly not identical with culture; they are independent of it. Yet the Kingdom of God comes to people who are profoundly linked to culture, and the building of the Kingdom cannot avoid borrowing elements of human cultures. (*Ecclesia in Asia,* n. 21)

159. As she carries out missionary activity among nations, the Church encounters different cultures and becomes involved in the process of inculturation.... She transmits to them her own values, at the same time taking the good elements that already exist in them and renewing them from within.
(*Redemptoris Missio,* n. 52)

160. ...[I]t is not possible to understand man on the basis of economics alone, nor to define him simply on the basis of class membership. Man is understood in a more complete way when he is situated within the sphere of culture through his language, history, and the position he takes towards the fundamental events of life, such as birth, love, work and death. At the heart of every culture lies the attitude man takes to the greatest mystery: the mystery of God.

Different cultures are basically different ways of facing the question of the meaning of personal existence. When this question is eliminated, the culture and moral life of nations are corrupted. (*Centesimus Annus*, n. 24)

IX. GENUINE HUMAN DEVELOPMENT

161. Increased possession is not the ultimate goal of nations nor of individuals. All growth is ambivalent. It is essential if man is to develop as a man, but in a way it imprisons man if he considers it the supreme good, and it restricts his vision. Then we see hearts harden and minds close, and men no longer gather together in friendship but out of self-interest, which soon leads to oppositions and disunity. The exclusive pursuit of possessions thus becomes an obstacle to individual fulfillment and to man's true greatness. Both for nations and for individual men, avarice is the most evident form of moral underdevelopment.
(*Populorum Progressio*, n. 19)

162. In brief, modern underdevelopment is not only economic but also cultural, political and simply human, as was indicated twenty years ago by the Encyclical *Populorum Progressio*. Hence at this point we have to ask ourselves if the sad reality of today might not be, at least in part, the result of a too narrow idea of development, that is, a mainly economic one.
(*Sollicitudo Rei Socialis*, n. 15)

163. Integral human development—the development of every person and of the whole person, especially of the poorest and most neglected in the community—is at the very heart of evangelization. Between evangelization and human development—development and

liberation—there are, in fact, profound links. These include links of an anthropological order, because man who is to be evangelized is not an abstract being but is subject to social and economic questions. (*Ecclesia in Africa*, n. 68)

164. The development of technology and the development of contemporary civilization, which is marked by the ascendancy of technology, demand a proportional development of morals and ethics. For the present, this last development seems unfortunately to be always left behind. Accordingly, in spite of the marvel of this progress, in which it is difficult not to see also authentic signs of man's greatness, signs that in their creative seeds were revealed to us in the pages of the book of Genesis, as early as where it describes man's creation, this progress cannot fail to give rise to disquiet on many counts. The first reason for disquiet concerns the essential and fundamental question: Does this progress, which has man for its author and promoter, make human life on earth 'more human' in every aspect of that life? Does it make it more 'worthy of man'? There can be no doubt that in various aspects it does. But the question keeps coming back with regard to what is most essential—whether in the context of this progress, man, as man, is becoming truly better, that is to say, more mature spiritually, more aware of the dignity of his humanity, more responsible, more open to others, especially the neediest and the weakest, and readier to give and to aid all. (*Redemptor Hominis*, n. 15)

165. At the same time, however, the 'economic' concept itself, linked to the word 'development,' has entered into crisis. In fact, there is a better understanding today that the mere accumulation of goods and services, even for the benefit of the majority, is not enough for the realization of human happiness. Nor, in consequence, does the availability of the many real benefits provided in recent times by

science and technology, including the computer sciences, bring freedom from slavery. On the contrary, the experience of recent years shows that unless all the considerable body of resources and potential at man's disposal is guided by a moral understanding and by an orientation towards the true good of the human race, it easily turns against man to oppress him.
(*Sollicitudo Rei Socialis*, n. 28)

166. If further development calls for the work of more and more technicians, even more necessary is the deep thought and reflection of wise men in search of a new humanism which will enable modern man to find himself anew by embracing the higher values of love and friendship, of prayer and contemplation. This is what will permit the fullness of authentic development, a development which is for each and all the transition from less human conditions to those which are more human.
(*Populorum Progressio*, n. 20)

X. THE COMMON GOOD

167. By the common good is to be understood "the sum total of social conditions which allow people, either as groups or as individuals, to reach their fulfillment more fully and more easily" (GS, n. 26). The common good concerns the life of all. It calls for prudence from each, and even more from those who exercise the office of authority. It consists of *three essential elements*:

First, the common good presupposes respect for the person as such. In the name of the common good, public authorities are bound to respect the fundamental and inalienable rights of the human person. Society should permit each of its members to fulfill his vocation. In particular, the common good resides in the conditions for the exercise of the natural freedoms indispensable for the development of the human vocation, such as "the right to act according to a sound norm of conscience and to safeguard ... privacy, and rightful freedom also in matters of religion" (GS, n. 26).

Second, the common good requires the social well-being and development of the group itself. Development is the epitome of all social duties. Certainly, it is the proper function of authority to arbitrate, in the name of the common good, between various particular interests; but it should make accessible to each what is needed to lead a truly human life: food, clothing, health, work, education and culture, suitable information, the right to establish a family, and so on.

Finally, the common good requires peace, that is, the stability and security of a just order. It presupposes that authority should ensure by morally acceptable means the security of society and its members. It is the basis of the right to legitimate personal and collective defense.

(CCC, nn. 1906–1909)

168. Every day, human interdependence grows more tightly drawn and spreads by degrees over the whole world. As a result, the common good, that is, the sum of those conditions of social life which allow social groups and their individual members relatively thorough and ready access to their own fulfillment, today takes on an increasingly universal complexion and consequently involves rights and duties with respect to the whole human race. Every social group must take account of the needs and legitimate aspirations of other groups, and even of the general welfare of the entire human family....

This social order requires constant improvement. It must be founded on truth, built on justice and animated by love; in freedom it should grow every day toward a more humane balance. An improvement in attitudes and abundant changes in society will have to take

place if these objectives are to be gained. God's Spirit, Who with a marvelous providence directs the unfolding of time and renews the face of the earth, is not absent from this development. The ferment of the Gospel, too, has aroused and continues to arouse in man's heart the irresistible requirements of his dignity.
(*Gaudium et Spes*, n. 26)

169. Authority is exercised legitimately only when it seeks the common good of the group concerned and if it employs morally licit means to attain it. If rulers were to enact unjust laws or take measures contrary to the moral order, such arrangements would not be binding in conscience. In such a case, "authority breaks down completely and results in shameful abuse" (PT, n. 51).
(CCC, n. 1903)

170. Moreover, if we carefully consider the essential nature of the common good on the one hand, and the nature and function of public authority on the other, everyone sees that there is an intrinsic connection between the two. And, indeed, just as the moral order needs public authority to promote the common good in civil society, it likewise demands that public authority actually be able to attain it. From this it follows that the governmental institutions, on which public authority depends and through which it functions and pursues its end, should be provided with such structure and efficacy that they can lead to the common good by ways and methods which are suitably adapted to various contingencies.
(*Pacem in Terris*, n. 136)

171. Considering the common good on the national level, the following points are relevant and should not be overlooked: to provide employment for as many workers as possible; to take care lest privileged groups arise even among the workers themselves; to main-

tain a balance between wages and prices; to make accessible the goods and services for a better life to as many persons as possible; either to eliminate or to keep within bounds the inequalities that exist between different sectors of the economy—that is, between agriculture, industry and services; to balance properly any increases in output with advances in services provided to citizens, especially by public authority; to adjust, as far as possible, the means of production to the progress of science and technology; finally, to ensure that the advantages of a more humane way of existence not merely subserve the present generation but have regard for future generations as well.

As regards the common good of human society as a whole, the following conditions should be fulfilled: that the competitive striving of peoples to increase output be free of bad faith; that harmony in economic affairs and a friendly and beneficial cooperation be fostered; and, finally, that effective aid be given in developing the economically underdeveloped nations.
(*Mater et Magistra*, nn. 79–80)

172. It is agreed that in our time the common good is chiefly guaranteed when personal rights and duties are maintained. The chief concern of civil authorities must therefore be to ensure that these rights are acknowledged, respected, coordinated with other rights, defended and promoted, so that in this way each one may more easily carry out his duties. For *to safeguard the inviolable rights of the human person, and to facilitate the fulfillment of his duties, should be the chief duty of every public authority.*
(*Pacem in Terris*, n. 60)

173. That these desired objectives be more readily obtained, it is necessary that public authorities have a correct understanding of the common good. This embraces the sum total of those conditions of social living, whereby men are enabled more fully and more readily

to achieve their own perfection. Hence, we regard it as necessary that the various intermediary bodies and the numerous social undertakings wherein an expanded social structure primarily finds expression, be ruled by their own laws, and as the common good itself progresses, pursue this objective in a spirit of sincere concord among themselves. Nor is it less necessary that the above mentioned groups present the form and substance of a true community. This they will do, only if individual members are considered and treated as persons, and are encouraged to participate in the affairs of the group.

Accordingly, as relationships multiply between men, binding them more closely together, commonwealths will more readily and appropriately order their affairs to the extent these two factors are kept in balance: (1) the freedom of individual citizens and groups of citizens to act autonomously, while cooperating one with the other; (2) the activity of the State whereby the undertakings of private individuals and groups are suitably regulated and fostered.
(*Mater et Magistra*, nn. 65–66)

174. It is also demanded by the common good that civil authorities should make earnest efforts to bring about a situation in which individual citizens can easily exercise their rights and fulfill their duties as well. For experience has taught us that, unless these authorities take suitable action with regard to economic, political, and cultural matters, inequalities between the citizens tend to become more and more widespread, especially in the modern world, and as a result human rights are rendered totally ineffective and the fulfillment of duties is compromised.
(*Pacem in Terris*, n. 63)

XI. "Social Sin"

175. Moreover, one must denounce the existence of economic, financial and social mechanisms which, although they are manipulated by people, often function almost automatically, thus accentuating the situation of wealth for some and poverty for the rest. These mechanisms, which are maneuvered directly or indirectly by the more developed countries, by their very functioning favor the interests of the people manipulating them. But in the end they suffocate or condition the economies of the less developed countries. Later on, these mechanisms will have to be subjected to a careful analysis under the ethical-moral aspect.
(*Sollicitudo Rei Socialis*, n. 16)

176. To speak of 'social sin' means in the first place to recognize that, by virtue of human solidarity, which is as mysterious and intangible as it is real and concrete, each individual's sin in some way affects others.... Some sins, however, by their very matter constitute a direct attack on one's neighbor and, more exactly, in the language of the Gospel, against one's brother or sister. They are an offense against God because they are offenses against one's neighbor. These sins are usually called 'social sins,' and this is the second meaning of the term.... Likewise, the term 'social' applies to every sin against justice in interpersonal relationships, committed either by the individual against the community or by the community against the individual.... Also social is every sin against the common good and its exigencies in relation to the whole broad spectrum of the rights and duties of citizens.
(*Reconciliatio et Paenitentia*, n. 16)

177. If the present situation can be attributed to difficulties of various kinds, it is not out of place to speak of structures of sin which, as I stated in my Apostolic Exhortation *Reconciliatio et Paenitentia*,

are rooted in personal sin, and thus always linked to the concrete acts of individuals who introduce these structures, consolidate them and make them difficult to remove. And thus they grow stronger, spread, and become the source of other sins, and so influence people's behavior.

(*Sollicitudo Rei Socialis*, n. 36)

I. TEMPORAL AUTHORITY

ARTICLE FIVE

THE ROLE OF THE STATE

178. "Human society can be neither well-ordered nor prosperous unless it has some people invested with legitimate authority to preserve its institutions and to devote themselves as far as is necessary to work and care for the good of all" (PT, n. 46).

By 'authority' one means the quality by virtue of which persons or institutions make laws and give orders to men and expect obedience from them.

Every human community needs an authority to govern it. The foundation of such authority lies in human nature. It is necessary for the unity of the state. Its role is to ensure as far as possible the common good of the society.

The authority required by the moral order derives from God: "Let every person be subject to the governing authorities. For there is no authority except from God, and those that exist have been instituted by God. Therefore he who resists the authorities resists what God has appointed, and those who resist will incur judgment" (Rom 13:1–2).

The duty of obedience requires all to give due honor to authority and to treat those who are charged to exercise it with respect, and, insofar as it is deserved, with gratitude and goodwill. Pope St. Clement of Rome provides the Church's most ancient prayer for political authorities: "Grant to them, Lord, health, peace, concord, and stability, so that they may exercise without offense the sovereignty that you have given them. Master, heavenly King of the ages, you give glory, honor, and power over the things of earth to the sons of men. Direct, Lord, their counsel, following what is pleasing and acceptable in your sight, so that by exercising with devotion and in peace and gentleness the power that you have given to them, they may find favor with you" (St. Clement of Rome, *Ad Cor*, n. 61).
(CCC, nn. 1897–1900)

179. It follows also that political authority, both in the commu-

nity as such and in the representative bodies of the state, must always be exercised within the limits of the moral order and directed toward the common good—with a dynamic concept of that good—according to the juridical order legitimately established or due to be established. When authority is so exercised, citizens are bound in conscience to obey. Accordingly, the responsibility, dignity and importance of leaders are indeed clear.
(*Gaudium et Spes*, n. 74)

180. Indeed it follows from the moral order itself that authority is necessary for civil society, for civil society is ruled by authority; and that authority cannot be used to thwart the moral order without instantly collapsing because its foundation has been destroyed. This is the warning of God Himself: "A word, then, for the kings' ears to hear, kings' hearts to heed: a message for you, rulers, wherever you be! Listen well, all you that have multitudes at your command, foreign hordes to do your bidding. Power is none but comes to you from the Lord, nor any royalty but from One who is above all. He it is that will call you to account for your doings with a scrutiny that reads your inmost thoughts" (Wis 6:1–4).
(*Pacem in Terris*, n. 83)

181. Authority does not derive its moral legitimacy from itself. It must not behave in a despotic manner, but must act for the common good as a "moral force based on freedom and a sense of responsibility" (GS, n. 74). "A human law has the character of law to the extent that it accords with right reason, and thus derives from the eternal law. Insofar as it falls short of right reason it is said to be an unjust law, and thus has not so much the nature of law as of a kind of violence" (Aquinas, *STh*, I–II, 93, 3, ad 3).
(CCC, n. 1902)

II. THE RULE OF LAW

182. The rule of law is the necessary condition for the establishment of an authentic democracy. For democracy to develop, there is a need for civic education and the promotion of public order and peace. In effect, there is no authentic and stable democracy without social justice. Thus the Church needs to pay greater attention to the formation of consciences, which will prepare the leaders of society for public life at all levels, promote civic education, respect for law and for human rights, and inspire greater efforts in the ethical training of political leaders.
(*Ecclesia in America*, n. 56)

183. But authority is not to be thought of as a force lacking all control. Indeed, since it is the power to command according to right reason, authority must derive its obligatory force from the moral order, which in turn has God for its first source and final end. Wherefore our Predecessor of happy memory, Pius XII, said: "The absolute order of living beings and man's very destiny (We are speaking of man who is free, bound by obligations and endowed with inalienable rights, and at once the basis of society and the purpose for which it exists) also includes the state as a necessary society invested with the authority without which it could not come into being or live.... And since this absolute order, as we learn from sound reason, and especially from the Christian faith, can have no origin save in God Who is our Creator, it follows that the dignity of the State's authority is due to its sharing to some extent in the authority of God Himself" (Pius XII, Christmas Eve Radio Message, 1944).
(*Pacem in Terris,* n. 47)

184. It is urgently necessary at this moment of history to strengthen juridical instruments capable of promoting freedom of conscience in the areas of political and social life. The gradual and

constant development of an internationally recognized legal order could well provide one of the surest bases for the peace and orderly progress of the human family. It is likewise essential that comparable efforts be undertaken nationally and regionally to ensure that all individuals, wherever they live, enjoy the protection of internationally recognized legal norms.
(*World Day of Peace Message*, 1991, n. 6)

185. Since the right to command is required by the moral order and has its source in God, it follows that, if civil authorities pass laws or command anything opposed to the moral order and, consequently, contrary to the will of God, neither the laws made nor the authorizations granted can be binding on the consciences of the citizens, since God has more right to be obeyed than men. Otherwise, authority breaks down completely and results in shameful abuse. As St. Thomas Aquinas teaches: "Human law has the true nature of law only in so far as it corresponds to right reason, and in this respect it is evident that it is derived from the eternal law. In so far as it falls short of right reason, a law is said to be a wicked law; and so, lacking the true nature of law, it is rather a kind of violence" (Aquinas, *STh*, I–II, 93, 3, ad 2).
(*Pacem in Terris,* n. 51)

186. Pope Leo XIII was aware of the need for a sound theory of the State in order to ensure the normal development of man's spiritual and temporal activities, both of which are indispensable. For this reason, in one passage of *Rerum Novarum* he presents the organization of society according to the three powers—legislative, executive and judicial—something which at the time represented a novelty in Church teaching. Such an ordering reflects a realistic vision of man's social nature, which calls for legislation capable of protecting the freedom of all. To that end, it is preferable that each

power be balanced by other powers and by other spheres of responsibility which keep it within proper bounds. This is the principle of the 'rule of law,' in which the law is sovereign, and not the arbitrary will of individuals.
(*Centesimus Annus*, n. 44)

187. It must also be restated that no social group, for example, a political party, has the right to usurp the role of sole leader, since this brings about the destruction of the true subjectivity of society and of the individual citizens, as happens in every form of totalitarianism.
(*Sollicitudo Rei Socialis*, n. 15)

III. THE ROLE OF GOVERNMENT

188. If, however, this political and juridical structure is to produce the advantages which may be expected of it, public officials must strive to meet the problems which arise in a way that conforms both to the complexities of the situation and the proper exercise of their function. This requires that, in constantly changing conditions, legislators never forget the norms of morality, or constitutional provisions, or the common good. Moreover, executive authorities must coordinate the activities of society with discretion, with a full knowledge of the law and after careful consideration of circumstances, and the courts must administer justice impartially and without being influenced by favoritism or pressure. The good order of society also demands that individual citizens and intermediate organizations should be effectively protected by law whenever they have rights to be exercised or obligations to be fulfilled.
(*Pacem in Terris*, n. 69)

189. This intervention of public authorities that encourages,

stimulates, regulates, supplements, and complements, is based on the principle of subsidiarity as set forth by Pius XI in his Encyclical *Quadragesimo Anno*: "It is a fundamental principle of social philosophy, fixed and unchangeable, that one should not withdraw from individuals and commit to the community what they can accomplish by their own enterprise and industry. So, too, it is an injustice and at the same time a grave evil and a disturbance of right order, to transfer to the larger and higher collectivity functions which can be performed and provided for by lesser and subordinate bodies. Inasmuch as every social activity should, by its very nature, prove a help to members of the body social, it should never destroy or absorb them" (QA, n. 23).
(*Mater et Magistra*, n. 53)

190. In the political sphere, it must be noted that truthfulness in the relations between those governing and those governed, openness in public administration, impartiality in the service of the body politic, respect for the rights of political adversaries, safeguarding the rights of the accused against summary trials and convictions, the just and honest use of public funds, the rejection of equivocal or illicit means in order to gain, preserve or increase power at any cost—all these are principles which are primarily rooted in, and in fact derive their singular urgency from, the transcendent value of the person and the objective moral demands of the functioning of States.
(*Veritatis Splendor*, n. 101)

IV. CHURCH AND STATE

191. The protection and promotion of the inviolable rights of man ranks among the essential duties of government. Therefore, government is to assume the safeguard of the religious freedom of all

its citizens, in an effective manner, by just laws and by other appropriate means. Government is also to help create conditions favorable to the fostering of religious life, in order that the people may be truly enabled to exercise their religious rights and to fulfill their religious duties, and also in order that society itself may profit by the moral qualities of justice and peace which have their origin in men's faithfulness to God and to His holy will.
(*Dignitatis Humanae*, n. 6)

V. FORMS OF GOVERNMENT

192. If authority belongs to the order established by God, "the choice of the political regime and the appointment of rulers are left to the free decision of the citizens" (GS, n. 74). The diversity of political regimes is morally acceptable, provided they serve the legitimate good of the communities that adopt them. Regimes whose nature is contrary to the natural law, to the public order, and to the fundamental rights of persons cannot achieve the common good of the nations on which they have been imposed.
(CCC, n. 1901)

193. In modern times, this concept has been opposed by totalitarianism, which, in its Marxist-Leninist form, maintains that some people, by virtue of a deeper knowledge of the laws of the development of society, or through membership of a particular class or through contact with the deeper sources of the collective consciousness, are exempt from error and can therefore arrogate to themselves the exercise of absolute power. It must be added that totalitarianism arises out of a denial of truth in the objective sense. If there is no transcendent truth, in obedience to which man achieves his full identity, then there is no sure principle for guaranteeing just relations between people.

Their self-interest as a class, group or nation would inevitably set them in opposition to one another. If one does not acknowledge transcendent truth, then the force of power takes over, and each person tends to make full use of the means at his disposal in order to impose his own interests or his own opinion, with no regard for the rights of others. People are then respected only to the extent that they can be exploited for selfish ends. Thus, the root of modern totalitarianism is to be found in the denial of the transcendent dignity of the human person who, as the visible image of the invisible God, is therefore by his very nature the subject of rights which no one may violate—no individual, group, class, nation or State. Not even the majority of a social body may violate these rights, by going against the minority, by isolating, oppressing, or exploiting it, or by attempting to annihilate it.

The culture and praxis of totalitarianism also involve a rejection of the Church. The State or the party which claims to be able to lead history towards perfect goodness, and which sets itself above all values, cannot tolerate the affirmation of an objective criterion of good and evil beyond the will of those in power, since such a criterion, in given circumstances, could be used to judge their actions. This explains why totalitarianism attempts to destroy the Church, or at least to reduce her to submission, making her an instrument of its own ideological apparatus.

Furthermore, the totalitarian State tends to absorb within itself the nation, society, the family, religious groups and individuals themselves. In defending her own freedom, the Church is also defending the human person, who must obey God rather than men (cf. Acts 5:29), as well as defending the family, the various social organizations and nations—all of which enjoy their own spheres of autonomy and sovereignty.

(*Centesimus Annus*, nn. 44–45)

194. In determining the structure and operation of government

which a State is to have, great weight has to be given to the circumstances of a given people, circumstances which will vary at different times and in different places. We consider, however, that it is in keeping with the innate demands of human nature that the State should take a form which embodies the three-fold division of powers corresponding to the three principal functions of public authority. In that type of State, not only the official functions of government but also the mutual relations between citizens and public officials are set down according to law, which in itself affords protection to the citizens both in the enjoyment of their rights and in the fulfillment of their duties. (*Pacem in Terris*, n. 68)

195. If the citizens' responsible cooperation is to produce the good results which may be expected in the normal course of political life, there must be a statute of positive law providing for a suitable division of the functions and bodies of authority and an efficient and independent system for the protection of rights. The rights of all persons, families and groups, and their practical application, must be recognized, respected and furthered, together with the duties binding on all citizens. Among the latter, it will be well to recall the duty of rendering the political community such material and personal service as are required by the common good. Rulers must be careful not to hamper the development of family, social or cultural groups, nor that of intermediate bodies or organizations, and not to deprive them of opportunities for legitimate and constructive activity; they should willingly seek, rather, to promote the orderly pursuit of such activity. Citizens, for their part, either individually or collectively, must be careful not to attribute excessive power to public authority, not to make exaggerated and untimely demands upon it in their own interests, lessening in this way the responsible role of persons, families and social groups. (*Gaudium et Spes*, n. 75)

196. When we speak of the reform of institutions, the State comes

chiefly to mind, not as if universal well-being were to be expected from its activity, but because things have come to such a pass through the evil of what we have termed 'individualism' that, following upon the overthrow and near extinction of that rich social life which was once highly developed through associations of various kinds, there remain virtually only individuals and the State. This is to the great harm of the State itself, for, with a structure of social governance lost, and with the taking over of all the burdens which the wrecked associations once bore, the State has been overwhelmed and crushed by almost infinite tasks and duties.
(*Quadragesimo Anno*, n. 78)

VI. Democracy

197. The Church values the democratic system inasmuch as it ensures the participation of citizens in making political choices, guarantees to the governed the possibility both of electing and holding accountable those who govern them, and of replacing them through peaceful means when appropriate. Thus she cannot encourage the formation of narrow ruling groups which usurp the power of the State for individual interests or for ideological ends.

Authentic democracy is possible only in a State ruled by law, and on the basis of a correct conception of the human person. It requires that the necessary conditions be present for the advancement both of the individual through education and formation in true ideals, and of the subjectivity of society through the creation of structures of participation and shared responsibility. Nowadays there is a tendency to claim that agnosticism and sceptical relativism are the philosophy and the basic attitude which correspond to democratic forms of political life.... It must be observed in this regard that if there is no ultimate truth to guide and direct political activity, then

ideas and convictions can easily be manipulated for reasons of power. As history demonstrates, a democracy without values easily turns into open or thinly disguised totalitarianism.
(*Centesimus Annus*, n. 46)

198. The Church respects the legitimate autonomy of the democratic order and is not entitled to express preferences for this or that institutional or constitutional solution. Her contribution to the political order is precisely her vision of the dignity of the person revealed in all its fullness in the mystery of the Incarnate Word.
(*Centesimus Annus*, n. 47)

199. Democracy cannot be idolized to the point of making it a substitute for morality or a panacea for immorality. Fundamentally, democracy is a 'system' and, as such, is a means and not an end. Its moral value is not automatic, but depends on conformity to the moral law to which it, like every other form of human behavior, must be subject: in other words, its morality depends on the morality of the ends which it pursues and of the means which it employs. If today we see an almost universal consensus with regard to the value of democracy, this is to be considered a positive 'sign of the times,' as the Church's Magisterium has frequently noted. But the value of democracy stands or falls with the values which it embodies and promotes.
(*Evangelium Vitae*, n. 70)

200. When these principles are not observed, the very basis of political coexistence is weakened, and the life of society itself is gradually jeopardized, threatened and doomed to decay (cf. Ps 14:3–4; Rv 18:2–3, 9–24). Today, when many countries have seen the fall of ideologies which bound politics to a totalitarian conception of the world—Marxism being the foremost of these—there is no less grave

a danger that the fundamental rights of the human person will be denied and that the religious yearnings which arise in the heart of every human being will be absorbed once again into politics. This is the risk of an alliance between democracy and ethical relativism, which would remove any sure moral reference point from political and social life, and, on a deeper level, make the acknowledgment of truth impossible. Indeed, "if there is no ultimate truth to guide and direct political activity, then ideas and convictions can easily be manipulated for reasons of power. As history demonstrates, a democracy without values easily turns into open or thinly disguised totalitarianism" (CA, n. 46). Thus, in every sphere of personal, family, social and political life, morality—founded upon truth and open in truth to authentic freedom—renders a primordial, indispensable and immensely valuable service not only for the individual person and his growth in the good, but also for society and its genuine development. (*Veritatis Splendor*, n. 101)

201. Only respect for life can be the foundation and guarantee of the most precious and essential goods of society, such as democracy and peace. There can be no true democracy without a recognition of every person's dignity and without respect for his or her rights. Nor can there be true peace unless life is defended and promoted. (*Evangelium Vitae*, n. 101)

ARTICLE SIX

THE ECONOMY

I. THE UNIVERSAL DESTINATION OF MATERIAL GOODS

202. "Fill the earth and subdue it" (Gn 1:28). The Bible, from the first page on, teaches us that the whole of creation is for man, that it is his responsibility to develop it by intelligent effort, and by means of his labor to perfect it, so to speak, for his use. If the world is made to furnish each individual with the means of livelihood and the instruments for his growth and progress, each man has, therefore, the right to find in the world what is necessary for himself. The recent Council reminded us of this: "God intended the earth and all that it contains for the use of every human being and people. Thus, as all men follow justice and unite in charity, created goods should abound for them on a reasonable basis" (GS, n. 69). All other rights whatsoever, including those of property and of free commerce, are to be subordinated to this principle. They should not hinder, but on the contrary, favor its application. It is a grave and urgent social duty to redirect them to their primary finality.
(*Populorum Progressio*, n. 22)

203. The Successors of Leo XIII have repeated this twofold affirmation: the necessity and therefore the legitimacy of private ownership, as well as the limits which are imposed on it. The Second Vatican Council likewise clearly restated the traditional doctrine in words which bear repeating: "In making use of the exterior things we lawfully possess, we ought to regard them not just as our own but also as common, in the sense that they can profit not only the owners but others too" (GS, n. 69); and a little later we read: "Private property or some ownership of external goods affords each person the scope needed for personal and family autonomy, and should be regarded as an extension of human freedom.... Of its nature, private property also has a social function

105

which is based on the law of the common purpose of goods" (GS, n. 71).
(*Centesimus Annus*, n. 30)

204. To own goods privately, as We saw above, is a right natural to man, and to exercise this right, especially in life in society, is not only lawful, but clearly necessary. "It is lawful for man to own his own things. It is even necessary for human life" (Aquinas, *STh*, II–II, 66, 2, c). But if the question be asked: How ought man to use his possessions? the Church replies without hesitation: "As to this point, man ought not regard external goods as his own, but as common so that, in fact, a person should readily share them when he sees others in need. Wherefore the Apostle says: 'Charge the rich of this world ... to give readily, to share with others'" (Aquinas, *STh*, II-II, 66, 2, c). No one, certainly, is obliged to assist others out of what is required for his own necessary use or for that of his family, or even to give to others what he himself needs to maintain his station in life becomingly and decently: "No one is obliged to live unbecomingly" (Aquinas, *STh*, II-II, 32, a. 6). But when the demands of necessity and propriety have been met, it is a duty to give to the poor out of that which remains. "Give that which remains as alms" (Lk 11:41). These are duties not of justice, except in cases of extreme need, but of Christian charity, which obviously cannot be enforced by legal action. But the laws and judgments of men yield precedence to the law and judgment of Christ the Lord, Who in many ways urges the practice of alms-giving: "It is more blessed to give than to receive" (Acts 20:35), and Who will judge a kindness done or denied to the poor as done or denied to Himself: "As long as you did it for one of these, the least of My brethren, you did it for Me" (Mt 25:40). The substance of all this is the following: whoever has received from the bounty of God a greater share of goods, whether corporeal and external, or of the soul, has received them for this purpose, namely, that he employ them for his

own perfection and, likewise, as a servant of Divine Providence, for the benefit of others. "Therefore, he that hath talent, let him constantly see to it that he be not silent; he that hath an abundance of goods, let him be on the watch that he grow not slothful in the generosity of mercy; he that hath a trade whereby he supports himself, let him be especially eager to share with his neighbor the use and benefit thereof" (St. Gregory the Great, *Evangelium Homiliae*, 9, 7). (*Rerum Novarum*, n. 22)

II. PRIVATE PROPERTY

205. The fact that God gave the whole human race the earth to use and enjoy cannot indeed in any manner serve as an objection against private possessions. For God is said to have given the earth to mankind in common, not because He intended indiscriminate ownership of it by all, but because He assigned no part to anyone in ownership, leaving the limits of private possessions to be fixed by the industry of men and the institutions of peoples. Yet, however the earth may be apportioned among private owners, it does not cease to serve the common interest of all, inasmuch as no living being is sustained except by what the fields bring forth. Those who lack resources supply labor, so that it can be truly affirmed that the entire scheme of securing a livelihood consists in the labor which a person expends either on his own land or in some working occupation, the compensation for which is drawn ultimately from no other source than from the varied products of the earth and is exchanged for them.

For this reason it also follows that private possessions are clearly in accord with nature. The earth indeed produces in great abundance the things to preserve and, especially, to perfect life, but of itself it could not produce them without human cultivation and care. (*Rerum Novarum*, nn. 8–9)

206. Accordingly, twin rocks of shipwreck must be carefully avoided. For, as one is wrecked upon, or comes close to, what is known as 'individualism' by denying or minimizing the social and public character of the right of property, so by rejecting or minimizing the private and individual character of this same right, one inevitably runs into 'collectivism' or at least closely approaches its tenets. Unless this is kept in mind, one is swept from his course upon the shoals of that moral, juridical, and social modernism which We denounced in the Encyclical (i.e., *Ubi Arcano Dei Consilio*) issued at the beginning of Our Pontificate. And, in particular, let those realize this who, in their desire for innovation, do not scruple to reproach the Church with infamous calumnies, as if she had allowed to creep into the teachings of her theologians a pagan concept of ownership which must be completely replaced by another that they with amazing ignorance call 'Christian'.
(*Quadragesimo Anno*, n. 46)

207. It is necessary to state once more the characteristic principle of Christian social doctrine: the goods of this world are originally meant for all. The right to private property is valid and necessary, but it does not nullify the value of this principle. Private property, in fact, is under a 'social mortgage,' which means that it has an intrinsically social function, based upon and justified precisely by the principle of the universal destination of material goods.
(*Sollicitudo Rei Socialis*, n. 42)

208. In the light of today's 'new things,' we have re-read *the relationship between individual or private property and the universal destination of material wealth*. Man fulfills himself by using his intelligence and freedom. In so doing he utilizes the things of this world as objects and instruments and makes them his own. The foundation of the right to private initiative and ownership is to be found

in this activity. By means of his work man commits himself, not only for his own sake but also *for others* and *with others*. Each person collaborates in the work of others and for their good. Man works in order to provide for the needs of his family, his community, his nation, and ultimately all humanity (*Laborem Exercens*, n. 10). Moreover, he collaborates in the work of his fellow employees, as well as in the work of suppliers and in the customers' use of goods, in a progressively expanding chain of solidarity. Ownership of the means of production, whether in industry or agriculture, is just and legitimate if it serves useful work. It becomes illegitimate, however, when it is not utilized or when it serves to impede the work of others, in an effort to gain a profit which is not the result of the overall expansion of work and the wealth of society, but rather is the result of curbing them or of illicit exploitation, speculation or the breaking of solidarity among working people (*Laborem Exercens*, n. 14). Ownership of this kind has no justification, and represents an abuse in the sight of God and man.
(*Centesimus Annus*, n. 43)

209. First, then, let it be considered as certain and established that neither Leo nor those theologians who have taught under the guidance and authority of the Church have ever denied or questioned the twofold character of ownership, called usually individual or social, according as it regards either separate persons or the common good. For they have always unanimously maintained that nature, rather than the Creator Himself, has given man the right of private ownership not only that individuals may be able to provide for themselves and their families but also that the goods which the Creator destined for the entire family of mankind may through this institution truly serve this purpose. All this can be achieved in no wise except through the maintenance of a certain and definite order.
(*Quadragesimo Anno,* n. 45)

III. ECONOMIC SYSTEMS

210. The Church has rejected the totalitarian and atheistic ideologies associated in modem times with 'communism' or 'socialism.' She has likewise refused to accept, in the practice of 'capitalism,' individualism and the absolute primacy of the law of the marketplace over human labor. Regulating the economy solely by centralized planning perverts the basis of social bonds; regulating it solely by the law of the marketplace fails social justice, for "there are many human needs which cannot be satisfied by the market" (CA, n. 34). Reasonable regulation of the marketplace and economic initiatives, in keeping with a just hierarchy of values and a view to the common good, is to be commended.
(CCC, n. 2425)

211. Returning now to the initial question: can it perhaps be said that, after the failure of Communism, capitalism is the victorious social system, and that capitalism should be the goal of the countries now making efforts to rebuild their economy and society? Is this the model which ought to be proposed to the countries of the Third World which are searching for the path to true economic and civil progress?

The answer is obviously complex. If by capitalism is meant an economic system which recognizes the fundamental and positive role of business, the market, private property, as well as free human creativity in the economic sector, then the answer is certainly in the affirmative, even though it would perhaps be more appropriate to speak of a 'business economy,' 'market economy,' or simply 'free economy'. But, if by 'capitalism' is meant a system in which freedom in the economic sector is not circumscribed within a strong juridical framework which places it at the service of human freedom in its totality and sees it as a particular aspect of that freedom, the core of which is ethical and religious, then the reply is certainly negative. (*Centesimus Annus*, n. 42)

212. The development of economic activity and growth in production are meant to provide for the needs of human beings. Economic life is not meant solely to multiply goods produced and increase profit or power; it is ordered first of all to the service of persons, of the whole man, and of the entire human community. Economic activity, conducted according to its own proper methods, is to be exercised within the limits of the moral order, in keeping with social justice so as to correspond to God's plan for man. (CCC, n. 2426)

213. It would appear that, on the level of individual nations and of international relations, the free market is the most efficient instrument for utilizing resources and effectively responding to needs. But this is true only for those needs which are 'solvent,' insofar as they are endowed with purchasing power, and for those resources which are 'marketable' insofar as they are capable of obtaining a satisfactory price. But there are many human needs which find no place on the market. It is a strict duty of justice and truth not to allow fundamental human needs to remain unsatisfied, and not to allow those burdened by such needs to perish. It is also necessary to help these needy people to acquire expertise, to enter the circle of exchange, and to develop their skills in order to make the best use of their capacities and resources. Even prior to the logic of a fair exchange of goods and the forms of justice appropriate to it, there exists something which is due to man because he is man, by reason of his lofty dignity. Inseparable from that required 'something' is the possibility to survive and, at the same time, to make an active contribution to the common good of humanity. In Third World contexts, certain objectives stated by *Rerum Novarum* remain valid, and, in some cases,

still constitute a goal yet to be reached, if a man's work and his very being are not to be reduced to the level of a mere commodity. These objectives include a sufficient wage for the support of the family, social insurance for old age and unemployment, and adequate protection for the conditions of employment.
(*Centesimus Annus*, n. 34)

214. It should also be noted that the justice of a socioeconomic system and, in each case, its just functioning, deserve in the final analysis to be evaluated by the way in which man's work is properly remunerated in the system. Here we return once more to the first principle of the whole ethical and social order, namely, the principle of the common use of goods. In every system, regardless of the fundamental relationships within it between capital and labor, wages, that is to say remuneration for work, are still a practical means whereby the vast majority of people can have access to those goods which are intended for common use: both the goods of nature and manufactured goods. Both kinds of goods become accessible to the worker through the wage which he receives as remuneration for his work. Hence, in every case, a just wage is the concrete means of verifying the justice of the whole socioeconomic system and, in any case, of checking that it is functioning justly. It is not the only means of checking, but it is a particularly important one and, in a sense, the key means.
(*Laborem Exercens,* n. 19)

215. In general, such attempts [to rebuild a democratic society inspired by social justice] endeavor to preserve free-market mechanisms, ensuring, by means of a stable currency and the harmony of social relations, the conditions for steady and healthy economic growth in which people, through their own work, can build a better future for themselves and their families. At the same time, these at-

tempts try to avoid making market mechanisms the only point of reference for social life, and they tend to subject them to public control, which upholds the principle of the common destination of material goods. In this context, an abundance of work opportunities, a solid system of social security and professional training, the freedom to join trade unions and the effective action of unions, the assistance provided in cases of unemployment, the opportunities for democratic participation in the life of society—all these are meant to deliver work from the mere condition of 'a commodity,' and to guarantee its dignity.
(*Centesimus Annus*, n. 19)

216. Attention must be given also to another matter that is closely connected with the foregoing. Just as the unity of human society cannot be founded on an opposition of classes, so also the right ordering of economic life cannot be left to a free competition of forces. For from this source, as from a poisoned spring, have originated and spread all the errors of individualist economic teaching. Destroying through forgetfulness or ignorance the social and moral character of economic life, it held that economic life must be considered and treated as altogether free from, and independent of, public authority, because in the market, i.e., in the free struggle of competitors, it would have a principle of self-direction which governs it much more perfectly than would the intervention of any created intellect. But free competition, while justified and certainly useful, provided it is kept within certain limits, clearly cannot direct economic life—a truth which the outcome of the application in practice of the tenets of this evil individualistic spirit has more than sufficiently demonstrated. Therefore, it is most necessary that economic life be again subjected to and governed by a true and effective directing principle. This function is one that the economic dictatorship which has recently displaced free competition can still less perform, since it is a headstrong

power and a violent energy that, to benefit people, needs to be strongly curbed and wisely ruled. But it cannot curb and rule itself. Loftier and nobler principles—social justice and social charity—must, therefore, be sought whereby this dictatorship may be governed firmly and fully. Hence, the institutions themselves of peoples and, particularly those of all social life, ought to be penetrated with this justice, and it is most necessary that it be truly effective, that is, establish a juridical and social order which will, as it were, give form and shape to all economic life. Social charity, moreover, ought to be as the soul of this order, an order which public authority ought to be ever ready effectively to protect and defend. It will be able to do this the more easily as it rids itself of those burdens which, as We have stated above, are not properly its own.
(*Quadragesimo Anno*, n. 88)

217. The modern business economy has positive aspects. Its basis is human freedom exercised in the economic field, just as it is exercised in many other fields. Economic activity is indeed but one sector in a great variety of human activities, and like every other sector, it includes the right to freedom, as well as the duty of making responsible use of freedom. But it is important to note that there are specific differences between the trends of modern society and those of the past, even the recent past. Whereas at one time the decisive factor of production was the land, and, later, capital—understood as a total complex of the instruments of production—today the decisive factor is increasingly man himself, that is, his knowledge, especially his scientific knowledge, his capacity for interrelated and compact organization, as well as his ability to perceive the needs of others and to satisfy them.
(*Centesimus Annus*, n. 32)

IV. MORALITY, JUSTICE, AND THE ECONOMIC ORDER

218. Even though economics and moral science each employs its own principles in its own sphere, it is, nevertheless, an error to say that the economic and moral orders are so distinct from and alien to each other that the former depends in no way on the latter. Certainly the laws of economics, as they are termed, being based on the very nature of material things and on the capacities of the human body and mind, determine the limits of what productive human effort cannot, and of what it can, attain in the economic field and by what means. Yet it is reason itself that clearly shows, on the basis of the individual and social nature of things and of men, the purpose which God ordained for all economic life.
(*Quadragesimo Anno*, n. 42)

219. Justice is to be observed not merely in the distribution of wealth, but also in regard to the conditions under which men engage in productive activity. There is, in fact, an innate need of human nature requiring that men engaged in productive activity have an opportunity to assume responsibility and to perfect themselves by their efforts.

Consequently, if the organization and structure of economic life be such that the human dignity of workers is compromised, or their sense of responsibility is weakened, or their freedom of action is removed, then we judge such an economic order to be unjust, even though it produces a vast amount of goods whose distribution conforms to the norms of justice and equity.
(*Mater et Magistra*, nn. 82–83)

220. Yet, if we look into the matter more carefully and more thoroughly, we shall clearly perceive that, preceding this ardently desired social restoration, there must be a renewal of the Christian

spirit, from which so many immersed in economic life have, far and wide, unhappily fallen away, lest all our efforts be wasted and our house be built not on a rock but on shifting sand.

And so, Venerable Brethren and Beloved Sons, having surveyed the present economic system, We have found it laboring under the gravest of evils. We have also summoned Communism and Socialism again to judgment and have found all their forms, even the most modified, to wander far from the precepts of the Gospel.
(*Quadragesimo Anno*, nn. 127–128)

221. I would like to invite economists and financial professionals, as well as political leaders, to recognize the urgency of the need to ensure that economic practices and related political policies have as their aim the good of every person and of the whole person. This is not only a demand of ethics but also a sound economy. Experience seems to confirm that economic success is increasingly dependent on a more genuine appreciation of individuals and their abilities, on their fuller participation, on their increased and improved knowledge and information, and on a stronger solidarity.
(*World Day of Peace Message*, 2000, n. 16)

222. Furthermore, the course of events thus far makes it clear that there cannot be a prosperous and well ordered society unless both private citizens and public authorities work together in economic affairs. Their activity should be characterized by mutual and amicable efforts, so that the roles assigned to each fit in with requirements of the common good, as changing times and customs suggest.
(*Mater et Magistra*, n. 56)

V. A Genuine Theology of Liberation

223. The Gospel of Jesus Christ is a message of freedom and a force for liberation. In recent years, this essential truth has become the object of reflection for theologians, with a new kind of attention which is itself full of promise. Liberation is first and foremost liberation from the radical slavery of sin. Its end and its goal is the freedom of the children of God, which is the gift of grace. As a logical consequence, it calls for freedom from many different kinds of slavery in the cultural, economic, social and political spheres, all of which derive ultimately from sin, and so often prevent people from living in a manner befitting their dignity.... Faced with the urgency of certain problems, some are tempted to emphasize, unilaterally, the liberation from servitude of an earthly and temporal kind. They do so in such a way that they seem to put liberation from sin in second place, and so fail to give it the primary importance it is due.
(*Libertatis Nuntius*, Introduction)

224. Faced with the urgency of sharing bread, some are tempted to put evangelization into parentheses, as it were, and postpone it until tomorrow: first the bread, then the Word of the Lord. It is a fatal error to separate these two, and even worse to oppose one to the other. In fact, the Christian perspective naturally shows they have a great deal to do with one another.
(*Libertatis Nuntius*, VI, n. 3)

225. To the extent that they remain fully Marxist, these currents continue to be based on certain fundamental tenets which are not compatible with the Christian conception of humanity and society.... Let us recall the fact that atheism and the denial of the human person, his liberty and his rights, are at the core of the Marxist theory. This theory, then, contains errors which directly threaten the truths

117

of the faith regarding the eternal destiny of individual persons. Moreover, to attempt to integrate into theology an analysis whose criterion of interpretation depends on this atheistic conception is to involve oneself in terrible contradictions.
(*Libertatis Nuntius*, VII, nn. 8–9)

226. We must not ignore the fact that many, even generous Christians who are sensitive to the dramatic questions involved in the problem of liberation, in their wish to commit the Church to the liberation effort are frequently tempted to reduce her mission to the dimensions of a simply temporal project. They would reduce her aims to a man-centered goal; the salvation of which she is the messenger would be reduced to material well-being. Her activity, forgetful of all spiritual and religious preoccupation, would become initiatives of the political or social order. But if this were so, the Church would lose her fundamental meaning. Her message of liberation would no longer have any originality and would easily be open to monopolization and manipulation by ideological systems and political parties.
(*Evangelii Nuntiandi*, n. 32)

227. Hence, when preaching liberation and associating herself with those who are working and suffering for it, the Church is certainly not willing to restrict her mission only to the religious field and dissociate herself from man's temporal problems. Nevertheless, she reaffirms the primacy of her spiritual vocation and refuses to replace the proclamation of the kingdom by the proclamation of forms of human liberation: she even states that her contribution to liberation is incomplete if she neglects to proclaim salvation in Jesus Christ.
(*Evangelii Nuntiandi*, n. 34)

228. The variety of situations and problems that exist in our world is indeed great and rapidly changing. For this reason it is all

the more necessary to guard against generalizations and unwarranted simplifications. It is possible, however, to highlight *some trends that are emerging in present-day society.* The gospel records that the weeds and the good grain grew together in the farmer's field. The same is true in history, where in everyday life there often exist contradictions in the exercise of human freedom, where there is found, side by side and at times closely intertwined, evil and good, injustice and justice, anguish and hope.
(Christifideles Laici, n. 3)

VI. STATE INTERVENTION AND THE ECONOMY

229. Another task of the State is that of overseeing and directing the exercise of human rights in the economic sector. However, primary responsibility in this area belongs not to the State but to individuals and to the various groups and associations which make up society. The State could not directly ensure the right to work for all its citizens unless it controlled every aspect of economic life and restricted the free initiative of individuals. This does not mean, however, that the State has no competence in this domain, as was claimed by those who argued against any rules in the economic sphere. Rather, the State has a duty to sustain business activities by creating conditions which will ensure job opportunities, by stimulating those activities where they are lacking or by supporting them in moments of crisis. The State has the further right to intervene when particular monopolies create delays or obstacles to development. In addition to the tasks of harmonizing and guiding development, in exceptional circumstances the State can also exercise a substitute function, when social sectors or business systems are too weak or are just getting underway, and are not equal to the task at hand. Such supplementary interventions, which are justified by urgent reasons touching the

common good, must be as brief as possible, so as to avoid removing permanently from society and business systems the functions which are properly theirs, and so as to avoid enlarging excessively the sphere of state intervention to the detriment of both economic and civil freedom.
(*Centesimus Annus*, n. 48)

230. Everyone has the right of economic initiative; everyone should make legitimate use of his talents to contribute to the abundance that will benefit all and to harvest the just fruits of his labor. He should seek to observe regulations issued by legitimate authority for the sake of the common good.
(CCC, n. 2429)

231. It is right to speak of a struggle against an economic system, if the latter is understood as a method of upholding the absolute predominance of capital, the possession of the means of production and of the land, in contrast to the free and personal nature of human work (cf. *Laborem Exercens*, n. 7). In the struggle against such a system, what is being proposed as an alternative is not the socialist system, which in fact turns out to be State capitalism, but rather *a society of free work, of enterprise and of participation.* Such a society is not directed against the market, but demands that the market be appropriately controlled by the forces of society and by the State, so as to guarantee that the basic needs of the whole of society are satisfied.
(*Centesimus Annus*, n. 35)

232. Individual initiative alone and the mere free play of competition could never assure successful development. One must avoid the risk of increasing still more the wealth of the rich and the dominion of the strong, whilst leaving the poor in their misery and adding

to the servitude of the oppressed. Hence programs are necessary in order "to encourage, stimulate, coordinate, supplement and integrate" (MM, n. 44) the activity of individuals and of intermediary bodies. It pertains to the public authorities to choose, even to lay down the objectives to be pursued, the ends to be achieved, and the means for attaining these, and it is for them to stimulate all the forces engaged in this common activity. But let them take care to associate private initiative and intermediary bodies with this work. They will thus avoid the danger of complete collectivization or of arbitrary planning, which, by denying liberty, would prevent the exercise of the fundamental rights of the human person.

(*Populorum Progressio*, n. 33)

233. Indeed, as is easily perceived, recent developments of science and technology provide additional reasons why, to a greater extent than heretofore, it is within the power of public authorities to reduce imbalances, whether these be between various sectors of economic life, or between different regions of the same nation, or even between different peoples of the world as a whole. These same developments make it possible to keep fluctuations in the economy within bounds, and to provide effective measures for avoiding mass unemployment. Consequently, it is requested again and again of public authorities responsible for the common good, that they intervene in a wide variety of economic affairs, and that, in a more extensive and organized way than heretofore, they adapt institutions, tasks, means, and procedures to this end.

(*Mater et Magistra*, n. 54)

234. At the outset it should be affirmed that in economic affairs first place is to be given to the private initiative of individual men who, either working by themselves, or with others in one fashion or another, pursue their common interests.

But in this matter, for reasons pointed out by our predecessors, it is necessary that public authorities take active interest, the better to increase output of goods and to further social progress for the benefit of all citizens.

This intervention of public authorities that encourages, stimulates, regulates, supplements, and complements, is based on the principle of subsidiarity as set forth by Pius XI in his Encyclical *Quadragesimo Anno*: "It is a fundamental principle of social philosophy, fixed and unchangeable, that one should not withdraw from individuals and commit to the community what they can accomplish by their own enterprise and industry. So, too, it is an injustice and at the same time a grave evil and a disturbance of right order, to transfer to the larger and higher collectivity functions which can be performed and provided for by lesser and subordinate bodies. Inasmuch as every social activity should, by its very nature, prove a help to members of the body social, it should never destroy or absorb them" (QA, n. 23).

(*Mater et Magistra*, nn. 51–53)

235. Socialization also presents dangers. Excessive intervention by the state can threaten personal freedom and initiative. The teaching of the Church has elaborated the principle of subsidiarity, according to which "a community of a higher order should not interfere in the internal life of a community of a lower order, depriving the latter of its functions, but rather should support it in case of need and help to co-ordinate its activity with the activities of the rest of society, always with a view to the common good" (CA, n. 48).

(CCC, n. 1883)

236. It is the task of the State to provide for the defense and preservation of common goods such as the natural and human environments, which cannot be safeguarded simply by market forces.

Just as in the time of primitive capitalism the State had the duty of defending the basic rights of workers, so now, with the new capitalism, the State and all of society have the duty of defending those collective goods which, among others, constitute the essential framework for the legitimate pursuit of personal goals on the part of each individual.
(*Centesimus Annus*, n. 40)

237. The principle of subsidiarity is opposed to all forms of collectivism. It sets limits for state intervention. It aims at harmonizing the relationships between individuals and societies. It tends toward the establishment of true international order.
(CCC, n. 1885)

238. These general observations also apply to the role of the State in the economic sector. Economic activity, especially the activity of a market economy, cannot be conducted in an institutional, juridical or political vacuum. On the contrary, it presupposes sure guarantees of individual freedom and private property, as well as a stable currency and efficient public services. Hence the principal task of the State is to guarantee this security, so that those who work and produce can enjoy the fruits of their labors and thus feel encouraged to work efficiently and honestly. The absence of stability, together with the corruption of public officials and the spread of improper sources of growing rich and of easy profits deriving from illegal or purely speculative activities, constitutes one of the chief obstacles to development and to the economic order.
(*Centesimus Annus*, n. 48)

239. In order to be fully effective, these efforts ought not remain scattered or isolated, much less be in competition for reasons of power or prestige: the present situation calls for concerted planning.

A planned program is of course better and more effective than occasional aid left to individual goodwill. It presupposes, as We said above, careful study, the selection of ends and the choice of means, as well as a reorganization of efforts to meet the needs of the present and the demands of the foreseeable future. More important, a concerted plan has advantages that go beyond the field of economic growth and social progress; for, in addition, it gives significance and value to the work undertaken. While shaping the world, it sets a higher value on man.

(*Populorum Progressio*, n. 50)

VII. BUSINESS

240. Mention has just been made of the fact that people work with each other, sharing in a 'community of work' which embraces ever widening circles. A person who produces something other than for his own use generally does so in order that others may use it after they have paid a just price, mutually agreed upon through free bargaining. It is precisely the ability to foresee both the needs of others and the combinations of productive factors most adapted to satisfying those needs that constitutes another important source of wealth in modern society. Besides, many goods cannot be adequately produced through the work of an isolated individual; they require the cooperation of many people in working towards a common goal. Organizing such a productive effort, planning its duration in time, making sure that it corresponds in a positive way to the demands which it must satisfy, and taking the necessary risks: all this, too, is a source of wealth in today's society. In this way, the role of disciplined and creative human work and, as an essential part of that work, initiative and entrepreneurial ability become increasingly evident and decisive.

This process, which throws practical light on a truth about the person which Christianity has constantly affirmed, should be viewed carefully and favorably. Indeed, besides the earth, man's principal resource is man himself. His intelligence enables him to discover the earth's productive potential and the many different ways in which human needs can be satisfied. It is his disciplined work in close collaboration with others that makes possible the creation of ever more extensive working communities which can be relied upon to transform man's natural and human environments. Important virtues are involved in this process, such as diligence, industriousness, prudence in undertaking reasonable risks, reliability and fidelity in interpersonal relationships, as well as courage in carrying out decisions which are difficult and painful but necessary, both for the overall working of a business and in meeting possible setbacks.
(*Centesimus Annus*, n. 32)

241. Without this consideration it is impossible to understand the meaning of the virtue of industriousness, and more particularly it is impossible to understand why industriousness should be a virtue: for virtue, as a moral habit, is something whereby man becomes good as man. This fact in no way alters our justifiable anxiety that in work, whereby matter gains in nobility, man himself should not experience a lowering of his own dignity. Again, it is well known that it is possible to use work in various ways against man, that it is possible to punish man with the system of forced labor in concentration camps, that work can be made into a means for oppressing man, and that in various ways it is possible to exploit human labor, that is to say, the worker. All this pleads in favor of the moral obligation to link industriousness as a virtue with the social order of work, which will enable man to become, in work, 'more a human being' and not be degraded by it, not only because of the wearing out of his physical strength (which, at least up to a certain point, is inevitable), but especially

125

through damage to the dignity and subjectivity that are proper to him.
(*Laborem Exercens*, n. 9)

242. The Church acknowledges the legitimate role of profit as an indication that a business is functioning well. When a firm makes a profit, this means that productive factors have been properly employed and corresponding human needs have been duly satisfied. But profitablility is not the only indicator of a firm's condition. It is possible for the financial accounts to be in order, and yet for the people—who make up the firm's most valuable asset—to be humiliated and their dignity offended ... Profit is a regulator of the life of a business, but it is not the only one; other human and moral factors must also be considered, which, in the long term, are at least equally important for the life of a business.
(*Centesimus Annus*, n. 35)

243. Everyone has the right of economic initiative; everyone should make legitimate use of his talents to contribute to the abundance that will benefit all and to harvest the just fruits of his labor. He should seek to observe regulations issued by legitimate authority for the sake of the common good.
(CCC, n. 2429)

244. The Church offers her social teaching as an *indispensable and ideal orientation*, a teaching which, as already mentioned, recognizes the positive value of the market and of enterprise, but which at the same time points out that these need to be oriented towards the common good. This teaching also recognizes the legitimacy of workers' efforts to obtain full respect for their dignity and to gain broader areas of participation in the life of industrial enterprises so that, while cooperating with others and under the direction of others, they can in

a certain sense "work for themselves" (cf. *Laborem Exercens*, n. 15) through the exercise of their intelligence and freedom. (*Centesimus Annus*, n. 43)

245. It should be noted that in today's world, among other rights, the right of economic initiative is often suppressed. Yet it is a right which is important not only for the individual but also for the common good. Experience shows us that the denial of this right, or its limitation in the name of an alleged 'equality' of everyone in society, diminishes, or, in practice, absolutely destroys the spirit of initiative, that is to say, the creative subjectivity of the citizen. As a consequence, there arises, not so much a true equality as a 'leveling down.' In the place of creative initiative there appears passivity, dependence and submission to the bureaucratic apparatus which, as the only 'ordering' and 'decision-making' body—if not also the 'owner'—of the entire totality of goods and the means of production, puts everyone in a position of almost absolute dependence, which is similar to the traditional dependence of the worker-proletarian in capitalism. This provokes a sense of frustration or desperation and predisposes people to opt out of national life, impelling many to emigrate and also favoring a form of 'psychological' emigration. (*Sollicitudo Rei Socialis*, n. 15)

246. Above all, it must be emphasized that enterprises and bodies of this sort, in order that they may survive and flourish, should be continuously adapted—both in their productive structure and in their operating methods—to new conditions of the times. These new conditions constantly arise from advances in science and technology, or from changing consumer needs and preferences. It is especially appropriate that all this be done by the craftsmen themselves and by the associates in the cooperatives. (*Mater et Magistra*, n. 87)

247. Nevertheless, to decide what is more helpful to the overall economic situation is not the prerogative of individual productive enterprises, but pertains to the public authorities and those institutions which, established either nationally or among a number of countries, function in various sectors of economic life. From this is evident the propriety or necessity of ensuring that not only managers or agents of management are represented before such authorities and institutions, but also workers or those who have the responsibility of safeguarding the rights, needs, and aspirations of workers.
(*Mater et Magistra*, n. 99)

VIII. ECONOMISM AND CONSUMERISM

248. What is in question is the advancement of persons, not just the multiplying of things that people can use. It is a matter—as a contemporary philosopher has said and as the Council has stated— not so much of 'having more' as of 'being more' (cf. GS, n. 35). Indeed, there is already a real perceptible danger that, while man's dominion over the world of things is making enormous advances, he should lose the essential threads of his dominion and in various ways let his humanity be subjected to the world and become himself something subject to manipulation in many ways—even if the manipulation is often not perceptible directly—through the whole organization of community life, through the production system and through pressure of the means of social communication. Man cannot relinquish himself or the place in the visible world that belongs to him; he cannot become the slave of things, the slave of economic systems, the slave of production, the slave of his own products.
(*Redemptor Hominis*, n. 16)

249. This superdevelopment, which consists in an excessive availability of every kind of material good for the benefit of certain social groups, easily makes people slaves of 'possession' and of immediate gratification, with no other horizon than the multiplication or continual replacement of the things already owned with others still better. This is the so-called civilization of 'consumption' or 'consumerism' which involves so much 'throwing away' and 'waste'.... To 'have' objects and goods does not in itself perfect the human subject, unless it contributes to the maturing and enrichment of that subject's 'being', that is to say, unless it contributes to realization of the human vocation as such.
(*Sollicitudo Rei Socialis*, n. 28)

250. To call for an existence which is qualitively more satisfying is of itself legitimate, but one cannot fail to draw attention to the new responsibilities and dangers connected with this phase of history. The manner in which new needs arise and are defined is always marked by a more or less appropriate concept of man and of his true good. A given culture reveals its overall understanding of life through the choices it makes in production and consumption. It is here that the phenomenon of consumerism arises. In singling out new needs and new means to meet them, one must be guided by a comprehensive picture of man which respects all the dimensions of his being and which subordinates his material and instinctive dimensions to his interior and spiritual ones.... It is not wrong to want to live better; what is wrong is a style of life which is presumed to be better when it is directed towards having rather than being and which wants to have more, not in order to be more, but in order to spend life in enjoyment as an end in itself.
(*Centesimus Annus*, n. 36)

ARTICLE SEVEN

WORK AND WAGES

I. THE NATURE OF WORK

251. The Church finds in the very first pages of the book of Genesis the source of her conviction that work is a fundamental dimension of human existence on earth. An analysis of these texts makes us aware that they express—sometimes in an archaic way of manifesting thought—the fundamental truths about man, in the context of the mystery of creation itself. These truths are decisive for man from the very beginning, and at the same time they trace out the main lines of his earthly existence, both in the state of original justice and also after the breaking, caused by sin, of the Creator's original covenant with creation in man. When man, who had been created "in the image of God ... male and female" (Gn 1:27), hears the words: "Be fruitful and multiply, and fill the earth and subdue it" (Gn 1:28–29), even though these words do not refer directly and explicitly to work, beyond any doubt they indirectly indicate it as an activity for man to carry out in the world. Indeed, they show its very deepest essence. Man is the image of God partly through the mandate received from his Creator to subdue, to dominate, the earth. In carrying out this mandate, man, every human being, reflects the very action of the Creator of the universe.

Work understood as a 'transitive' activity, that is to say, an activity beginning in the human subject and directed towards an external object, presupposes a specific dominion by man over 'the earth,' and in its turn it confirms and develops this dominion. It is clear that the term 'the earth' of which the biblical text speaks is to be understood in the first place as that fragment of the visible universe that man inhabits. By extension, however, it can be understood as the whole of the visible world insofar as it comes within the range of man's influence and of his striving to satisfy his needs. The expression 'subdue the earth' has an immense range. It means all the resources that the earth (and, indirectly, the visible world) contains and which,

133

through the conscious activity of man, can be discovered and used for his ends. And so these words, placed at the beginning of the Bible, never cease to be relevant. They embrace equally the past ages of civilization and economy, as also the whole of modern reality and future phases of development, which are perhaps already to some extent beginning to take shape, though for the most part they are still almost unknown to man and hidden from him.
(*Laborem Exercens*, n. 4)

252. In our time, *the role of human work* is becoming increasingly important as the productive factor both of non-material and of material wealth. Moreover, it is becoming clearer how a person's work is naturally interrelated with the work of others. More than ever, *work is work with others* and *work for others*: it is a matter of doing something for someone else. Work becomes ever more fruitful and productive to the extent that people become more knowledgeable of the productive potentialities of the earth and more profoundly cognizant of the needs of those for whom their work is done.
(*Centesimus Annus*, n. 31)

253. In the design of God, every man is called upon to develop and fulfill himself, for every life is a vocation. At birth, everyone is granted, in germ, a set of aptitudes and qualities for him to bring to fruition. Their coming to maturity, which will be the result of education received from the environment and personal efforts, will allow each man to direct himself toward the destiny intended for him by his Creator. Endowed with intelligence and freedom, he is responsible for his fulfillment, as he is for his salvation. He is aided, or sometimes impeded, by those who educate him and those with whom he lives, but each one remains, whatever be these influences affecting him, the principal agent of his own success or failure. By the unaided effort of his own intelligence and his will, each man can

grow in humanity, can enhance his personal worth, can become more a person.
(*Populorum Progressio*, n. 15)

254. Human work proceeds directly from persons created in the image of God and called to prolong the work of creation by subduing the earth, both with and for one another. Hence work is a duty: "If any one will not work, let him not eat" (2 Thes 3:10). Work honors the Creator's gifts and the talents received from him. It can also be redemptive. By enduring the hardship of work in union with Jesus, the carpenter of Nazareth and the one crucified on Calvary, man collaborates in a certain fashion with the Son of God in his redemptive work. He shows himself to be a disciple of Christ by carrying the cross, daily, in the work he is called to accomplish. Work can be a means of sanctification and a way of animating earthly realities with the Spirit of Christ.
(CCC, n. 2427)

255. Throughout the course of the centuries, men have labored to better the circumstances of their lives through a monumental amount of individual and collective effort. To believers, this point is settled: considered in itself, such human activity accords with God's will. For man, created to God's image, received a mandate to subject to himself the earth and all that it contains, and to govern the world with justice and holiness, a mandate to relate himself and the totality of things to Him, who was acknowledged as the Lord and Creator of all.
(*Gaudium et Spes*, n. 34)

256. Man has to subdue the earth and dominate it, because as the 'image of God' he is a person, that is to say, a subjective being capable of acting in a planned and rational way, capable of deciding

about himself, and with a tendency to self-realization. As a person, man is therefore the subject of work. As a person, he works, he performs various actions belonging to the work process; independently of their objective content, these actions must all serve to realize his humanity, to fulfill the calling to be a person that is his by reason of his very humanity.
(*Laborem Exercens*, n. 6)

257. Man must work, both because the Creator has commanded it and because of his own humanity, which requires work in order to be maintained and developed. Man must work out of regard for others, especially his own family, but also for the society he belongs to, the country of which he is a child, and the whole human family of which he is a member, since he is the heir to the work of generations and at the same time a sharer in building the future of those who will come after him in the succession of history. All this constitutes the moral obligation of work, understood in its wide sense. When we have to consider the moral rights, corresponding to this obligation, of every person with regard to work, we must always keep before our eyes the whole vast range of points of reference in which the labor of every working subject is manifested.
(*Laborem Exercens*, n. 16)

II. JUST WAGES AND COMPENSATION

258. Among the most important duties of employers, the principal one is to give every worker what is justly due him. Assuredly, to establish a rule of pay in accord with justice, many factors must be taken into account. But, in general, the rich and employers must remember that no laws, either human or divine, permit them for their own profit to oppress the needy and the wretched or to seek gain

from another's want. To defraud anyone of the wage due him is a great crime that calls down avenging wrath from Heaven: "Behold, the wages of the laborers ... which have been kept back by you unjustly, cry out: and their cry has entered into the ears of the Lord of Hosts" (Jas 5:4). Finally, the rich must religiously avoid harming in any way the savings of the workers, either by coercion, or by fraud, or by the arts of usury; and the more for this reason, that the workers are not sufficiently protected against injustices and violence, and their property, being so meager, ought to be regarded as all the more sacred. Could not the observance alone of the foregoing laws remove the bitterness and the causes of the conflict?
(*Rerum Novarum*, n. 20)

259. In determining the amount of the wage, the condition of a business and of the one carrying it on must also be taken into account; for it would be unjust to demand excessive wages which a business cannot stand without its ruin and consequent calamity to the workers. If, however, a business makes too little money, because of lack of energy or lack of initiative or because of indifference to technical and economic progress, that must not be regarded a just reason for reducing the compensation of the workers. But if the business in question is not making enough money to pay the workers an equitable wage because it is being crushed by unjust burdens or forced to sell its product at less than a just price, those who are thus the cause of the injury are guilty of grave wrong, for they deprive workers of their just wage and force them under the pinch of necessity to accept a wage less than fair.
(*Quadragesimo Anno*, n. 72)

260. It also seems necessary to make provision for a twofold insurance, one covering agricultural output, the other covering farmers and their families. Because, as experience shows, the income of

individual farmers is, on the average, less than that of workers in industry and the services, it does not seem to be fully in accord with the norms of social justice and equity to provide farmers with insurance or social security benefits that are inferior to those of other classes of citizens. For those insurance plans or provisions that are established generally should not differ markedly one from the other, whatever be the economic sector wherein the citizens work, or from which they derive their income.
(*Mater et Magistra*, n. 135)

261. Besides wages, various social benefits intended to ensure the life and health of workers and their families play a part here. The expenses involved in health care, especially in the case of accidents at work, demand that medical assistance should be easily available for workers, and that, as far as possible, it should be cheap or even free of charge. Another sector regarding benefits is the sector associated with the right to rest. In the first place, this involves a regular weekly rest comprising at least Sunday, and also a longer period of rest, namely the holiday or vacation taken once a year or possibly in several shorter periods during the year. A third sector concerns the right to a pension and to insurance for old age and in case of accidents at work. Within the sphere of these principal rights, there develops a whole system of particular rights which, together with remuneration for work, determine the correct relationship between worker and employer. Among these rights, there should never be overlooked the right to a working environment and to manufacturing processes which are not harmful to the workers' physical health or to their moral integrity.
(*Laborem Exercens*, n. 19)

262. In the first place, the worker must be paid a wage sufficient to support him and his family. That the rest of the family should also

contribute to the common support, according to the capacity of each, is certainly right, as can be observed especially in the families of farmers, but also in the families of many craftsmen and small shopkeepers. But to abuse the years of childhood and the limited strength of women is grossly wrong. Mothers, concentrating on household duties, should work primarily in the home or in its immediate vicinity. It is an intolerable abuse, and to be abolished at all cost, for mothers, on account of the father's low wage, to be forced to engage in gainful occupations outside the home to the neglect of their proper cares and duties, especially the training of children. Every effort must therefore be made that fathers of families receive a wage large enough to meet ordinary family needs adequately. But if this cannot always be done under existing circumstances, social justice demands that changes be introduced as soon as possible whereby such a wage will be assured to every adult working man. It will not be out of place here to render merited praise to all, who with a wise and useful purpose, have tried and tested various ways of adjusting the pay for work to family burdens in such a way that, as these increase, the former may be raised and, indeed, if the contingency arises, there may be enough to meet extraordinary needs.
(*Quadragesimo Anno*, n. 71)

263. A just wage is the legitimate fruit of work. To refuse or withhold it can be a grave injustice. In determining fair pay, both the needs and the contributions of each person must be taken into account. "Remuneration for work should guarantee man the opportunity to provide a dignified livelihood for himself and his family on the material, social, cultural and spiritual level, taking into account the role and the productivity of each, the state of the business, and the common good" (GS, n. 67). Agreement between the parties is not sufficient to justify morally the amount to be received in wages. (CCC, n. 2434)

264. Finally, remuneration for labor is to be such that man may be furnished the means to cultivate worthily his own material, social, cultural, and spiritual life and that of his dependents, in view of the function and productiveness of each one, the conditions of the factory or workshop, and the common good.
(*Gaudium et Spes*, n. 67)

265. We shall now touch upon a matter of very great importance, and one which must be correctly understood in order to avoid falling into error on one side or the other. We are told that free consent fixes the amount of a wage; that, therefore, the employer, after paying the wage agreed to would seem to have discharged his obligation and not to owe anything more; that only then would injustice be done if either the employer should refuse to pay the whole amount of the wage, or the worker should refuse to perform all the work to which he had committed himself; and that in those cases, but in no others, is it proper for the public authority to safeguard the rights of each party.
(*Rerum Novarum*, n. 43)

266. Let it be granted, then, that worker and employer may enter freely into agreements and, in particular, concerning the amount of the wage; yet there is always underlying such agreements an element of natural justice, and one greater and more ancient than the free consent of contracting parties, namely, that the wage shall not be less than enough to support a worker who is thrifty and upright. If, compelled by necessity or moved by fear of a worse evil, a worker accepts a harder condition, which, although against his will he must accept because an employer or contractor imposes it, he certainly submits to force, against which justice cries out in protest.
(*Rerum Novarum*, n. 45)

267. Furthermore, society and the State must ensure wage levels adequate for the maintenance of the worker and his family, including a certain amount for savings. This requires a continuous effort to improve workers' training and capability so that their work will be more skilled and productive, as well as careful controls and adequate legislative measures to block shameful forms of exploitation, especially to the disadvantage of the most vulnerable workers, of immigrants and of those on the margins of society. The role of trade unions in negotiating minimum salaries and working conditions is decisive in this area.
(*Centesimus Annus*, n. 15)

III. THE WORK PLACE

268. Work, of course, can have contrary effects, for it promises money, pleasure and power, invites some to selfishness, others to revolt; it also develops professional awareness, sense of duty and charity to one's neighbor. When it is more scientific and better organized, there is a risk of its dehumanizing those who perform it, by making them its servants, for work is human only if it remains intelligent and free. John XXIII gave a reminder of the urgency of giving everyone who works his proper dignity by making him a true sharer in the work he does with others: "every effort should be made that the enterprise become a community of persons in the dealings, activities and standing of all its members" (MM, n. 91). Man's labor means much more still for the Christian: the mission of sharing in the creation of the supernatural world, which remains incomplete until we all come to build up together that perfect Man of whom St. Paul speaks, "who realizes the fullness of Christ" (Eph 4:13).
(*Populorum Progressio*, n. 28)

269. This requires that mutual relations between employers and directors, on the one hand, and the employees of the enterprise, on the other, be marked by mutual respect, esteem, and good will. It also demands that all collaborate sincerely and harmoniously in their joint undertaking, and that they perform their work not merely with the objective of deriving an income, but also of carrying out the role assigned them and of performing a service that results in benefit to others. This means that the workers may have a say in, and may make a contribution toward, the efficient running and development of the enterprise. Thus, our predecessor of happy memory, Pius XII, clearly indicated: "The economic and social functions which everyone aspires to fulfill, require that efforts of individuals be not wholly subjected to the will of others" (Allocution, 1956). Beyond doubt, an enterprise truly in accord with human dignity should safeguard the necessary and efficient unity of administration. But it by no means follows that those who work daily in such an enterprise are to be considered merely as servants, whose sole function is to execute orders silently, and who are not allowed to interject their desires and interests, but must conduct themselves as idle standbys when it comes to assignment and direction of their tasks.
(*Mater et Magistra*, n. 92)

270. Finally, 'humane' working hours and adequate freetime need to be guaranteed, as well as the right to express one's own personality at the workplace without suffering any affront to one's conscience or personal dignity. This is the place to mention once more the role of trade unions, not only in negotiating contracts, but also as 'places' where workers can express themselves. They serve the development of an authentic culture of work and help workers to share in a fully human way in the life of their place of employment.
(*Centesimus Annus*, n. 15)

271. The following duties, on the other hand, concern rich men and employers: Workers are not to be treated as slaves; justice demands that the dignity of human personality be respected in them, ennobled as it has been through what we call the Christian character. If we hearken to natural reason and to Christian philosophy, gainful occupations are not a mark of shame to man, but rather of respect, as they provide him with an honorable means of supporting life. It is shameful and inhuman, however, to use men as things for gain and to put no more value on them than what they are worth in muscle and energy. Likewise, it is enjoined that the religious interests and the spiritual well-being of the workers receive proper consideration. Wherefore, it is the duty of employers to see that the worker is free for adequate periods to attend to his religious obligations; not to expose anyone to corrupting influences or the enticements of sin; and in no way to alienate him from care for his family and the practice of thrift. Likewise, more work is not to be imposed than strength can endure, nor that kind of work which is unsuited to a worker's age or sex.

(*Rerum Novarum*, n. 20)

272. Therefore the Church can and should help modern society by tirelessly insisting that the work of women in the home be recognized and respected by all in its irreplaceable value. This is of particular importance in education: for possible discrimination between the different types of work and professions is eliminated at its very root once it is clear that all people, in every area, are working with equal rights and equal responsibilities. The image of God in man and in woman will thus be seen with added luster. While it must be recognized that women have the same right as men to perform various public functions, society must be structured in such a way that wives and mothers are not in practice compelled to work outside the home, and that their families can live and prosper in a dignified way, even

when they themselves devote their full time to their own family. Furthermore, the mentality which honors women more for their work outside the home than for their work within the family must be overcome. This requires that men should truly esteem and love women with total respect for their personal dignity, and that society should create and develop conditions favoring work in the home.
(*Familiaris Consortio*, n. 23)

273. Similarly with work: while it can sometimes be given exaggerated significance, it is for all something willed and blessed by God. Man created to His image "must cooperate with his Creator in the perfecting of creation and communicate to the earth the spiritual imprint he himself has received" (Paul VI, *Letter to the Fifty-First Session of the French Social Weeks*). God, Who has endowed man with intelligence, imagination and sensitivity, has also given him the means of completing His work in a certain way: whether he be artist or craftsman, engaged in management, industry or agriculture, everyone who works is a creator. Bent over a material that resists his efforts, a man by his work gives his imprint to it, acquiring, as he does so, perseverance, skill and a spirit of invention. Further, when work is done in common, when hope, hardship, ambition and joy are shared, it brings together and firmly unites the wills, minds and hearts of men: in its accomplishment, men find themselves to be brothers.
(*Populorum Progressio*, n. 27)

IV. UNEMPLOYMENT

274. When we consider the rights of workers in relation to the 'indirect employer,' that is to say, all the agents at the national and international level that are responsible for the whole orientation of labor policy, we must first direct our attention to a fundamental is-

sue: the question of finding work, or, in other words, the issue of suitable employment for all who are capable of it. The opposite of a just and right situation in this field is unemployment, that is to say, the lack of work for those who are capable of it. It can be a question of general unemployment or of unemployment in certain sectors of work. The role of the agents included under the title of indirect employer is to act against unemployment, which in all cases is an evil, and which, when it reaches a certain level, can become a real social disaster. It is particularly painful when it especially affects young people, who, after appropriate cultural, technical and professional preparation, fail to find work, and see their sincere wish to work and their readiness to take on their own responsibility for the economic and social development of the community sadly frustrated. The obligation to provide unemployment benefits, that is to say, the duty to make suitable grants indispensable for the subsistence of unemployed workers and their families, is a duty springing from the fundamental principle of the moral order in this sphere, namely the principle of the common use of goods or, to put it in another and still simpler way, the right to life and subsistence.
(*Laborem Exercens,* n. 18)

275. Access to employment and to professions must be open to all without unjust discrimination: men and women, healthy and disabled, natives and immigrants. For its part, society should, according to circumstances, help citizens find work and employment. (CCC, n. 2433)

276. Beginning our discussion of the rights of man, we see that every man has the right to life, to bodily integrity, and to the means which are suitable for the proper development of life; these are primarily food, clothing, shelter, rest, medical care, and, finally, the necessary social services. Therefore, a human being also has the right

to security in cases of sickness, inability to work, widowhood, old age, unemployment, or in any other case in which he is deprived of the means of subsistence through no fault of his own.
(*Pacem in Terris*, n. 11)

V. Unions

277. From the fact that human beings are by nature social, there arises the right of assembly and association. They have also the right to give the societies of which they are members the form they consider most suitable for the aim they have in view, and to act within such societies on their own initiative and on their own responsibility in order to achieve their desired objectives.
(*Pacem in Terris*, n. 23)

278. The rules, therefore, which Leo XIII issued in virtue of his authority, deserve the greatest praise in that they have been able to break down this hostility and dispel these suspicions; but they have even a higher claim to distinction in that they encouraged Christian workers to found mutual associations according to their various occupations, taught them how to do so, and resolutely confirmed in the path of duty a goodly number of those whom socialist organizations strongly attracted by claiming to be the sole defenders and champions of the lowly and oppressed.

With respect to the founding of these societies, the Encyclical *On the Condition of Workers* most fittingly declared that "workers' associations ought to be so constituted and so governed as to furnish the most suitable and most convenient means to attain the object proposed, which consists in this, that the individual members of the association secure, so far as is possible, an increase in the goods of body, of soul, and of property" (RN, n. 53), yet it is clear that "moral

and religious perfection ought to be regarded as their principal goal, and that their social organization as such ought above all to be directed completely by this goal" (RN, n. 53). For "when the regulations of associations are founded upon religion, the way is easy toward establishing the mutual relations of the members, so that peaceful living together and prosperity will result" (RN, n. 54).
(*Quadragesimo Anno*, nn. 31–32)

279. Labor which is too long and too hard, and the belief that pay is inadequate, not infrequently give workers cause to strike and become voluntarily idle. This evil, which is frequent and serious, ought to be remedied by public authority, because such interruption of work inflicts damage not only upon employers and upon the workers themselves, but also injures trade and commerce and the general interests of the State; and, since it is usually not far removed from violence and rioting, it very frequently jeopardizes public peace. In this matter it is more effective and salutary that the authority of the law anticipate and completely prevent the evil from breaking out by removing early the causes from which it would seem that conflict between employers and workers is bound to arise.
(*Rerum Novarum,* n. 39)

280. In the task of development, man, who finds his life's primary environment in the family, is often aided by professional organizations. If it is their objective to promote the interests of their members, their responsibility is also great with regard to the educative task which at the same time they can and ought to accomplish. By means of the information they provide and the formation they propose, they can do much to give to all a sense of the common good and of the consequent obligations that fall upon each person.
(*Populorum Progressio*, n. 38)

281. All these rights, together with the need for the workers themselves to secure them, give rise to yet another right: the right of association, that is, to form associations for the purpose of defending the vital interests of those employed in the various professions. These associations are called labor or trade unions. The vital interests of the workers are to a certain extent common for all of them; at the same time, however, each type of work, each profession, has its own specific character which should find a particular reflection in these organizations.
(*Laborem Exercens*, n. 20)

282. Among the basic rights of the human person is to be numbered the right of freely founding unions for working people. These should be able truly to represent them and to contribute to the organizing of economic life in the right way. Included is the right of freely taking part in the activity of these unions without risk of reprisal. Through this orderly participation joined to progressive economic and social formation, all will grow day by day in the awareness of their own function and responsibility, and thus they will be brought to feel that they are comrades in the whole task of economic development and in the attainment of the universal common good according to their capacities and aptitudes.
(*Gaudium et Spes*, n. 68)

283. The civil authority itself constitutes the syndicate as a juridical personality in such a manner as to confer on it simultaneously a certain monopoly-privilege, since only such a syndicate, when thus approved, can maintain the rights (according to the type of syndicate) of workers or employers, and since it alone can arrange for the placement of labor and conclude so-termed labor agreements. Anyone is free to join a syndicate or not, and only within these limits can this kind of syndicate be called free; for syndical dues and special

assessments are exacted of absolutely all members of every speci-
fied calling or profession, whether they are workers or employers;
likewise, all are bound by the labor agreements made by the legally
recognized syndicate. Nevertheless, it has been officially stated that
this legally recognized syndicate does not prevent the existence, without legal status, however, of other associations made up of persons
following the same calling.
(*Quadragesimo Anno*, n. 92)

VI. STRIKES

284. Recourse to a strike is morally legitimate when it cannot
be avoided, or at least when it is necessary to obtain a proportionate
benefit. It becomes morally unacceptable when accompanied by violence, or when objectives are included that are not directly linked to
working conditions or are contrary to the common good.
(CCC, n. 2435)

285. One method used by unions in pursuing the just rights of
their members is the strike or work stoppage, as a kind of ultimatum
to the competent bodies, especially the employers. This method is
recognized by Catholic social teaching as legitimate in the proper
conditions and within just limits. In this connection, workers should
be assured the right to strike, without being subjected to personal
penal sanctions for taking part in a strike. While admitting that it is a
legitimate means, we must at the same time emphasize that a strike
remains, in a sense, an extreme means. It must not be abused; it must
not be abused especially for 'political' purposes. Furthermore, it must
never be forgotten that, when essential community services are in
question, they must in every case be ensured, if necessary, by means
of appropriate legislation. Abuse of the strike weapon can lead to the

paralysis of the whole of socioeconomic life, and this is contrary to the requirements of the common good of society, which also corresponds to the properly understood nature of work itself.
(*Laborem Exercens,* n. 20)

286. When, however, socio-economic disputes arise, efforts must be made to come to a peaceful settlement. Although recourse must always be had first to a sincere dialogue between the parties, a strike, nevertheless, can remain even in present day circumstances a necessary, though ultimate, aid for the defense of the workers' own rights and the fulfillment of their just desires. As soon as possible, however, ways should be sought to resume negotiation and the discussion of reconciliation.
(*Gaudium et Spes*, n. 68)

ARTICLE EIGHT

POVERTY AND CHARITY

I. THE SCANDAL OF POVERTY

287. For this reason, I wish to call attention to a number of general indicators, without excluding other specific ones. Without going into an analysis of figures and statistics, it is sufficient to face squarely the reality of an innumerable multitude of people—children, adults and the elderly—in other words, real and unique human persons, who are suffering under the intolerable burden of poverty. There are many millions who are deprived of hope due to the fact that, in many parts of the world, their situation has noticeably worsened. Before these tragedies of total indigence and need, in which so many of our brothers and sisters are living, it is the Lord Jesus himself who comes to question us (cf. Mt 25:31–46).
(*Sollicitudo Rei Socialis*, n. 13)

288. Looking at all the various sectors—the production and distribution of foodstuffs, hygiene, health and housing, availability of drinking water, working conditions (especially for women), life expectancy and other economic and social indicators—the general picture is a disappointing one, both considered in itself and in relation to the corresponding data of the more developed countries. The word 'gap' returns spontaneously to mind.
(*Sollicitudo Rei Socialis*, n. 14)

289. Those who lack fortune's goods are taught by the Church that, before God as judge, poverty is no disgrace, and that no one should be ashamed because he makes his living by toil. And Jesus Christ has confirmed this by fact and by deed, Who for the salvation of men, "being rich, became poor" (2 Cor 8:9) and, although He was the Son of God and God Himself, yet He willed to seem and to be thought the son of a carpenter; nay, He even did not disdain to spend a great part of his life at the work of a carpenter. "Is not this the

carpenter, the Son of Mary?" (Mk 6:3) Those who contemplate this Divine example will more easily understand these truths: True dignity and excellence in men resides in moral living, that is, in virtue; virtue is the common inheritance of man, attainable equally by the humblest and the mightiest, by the rich and the poor; and the reward of eternal happiness will follow upon virtue and merit alone, regardless of the person in whom they may be found. Nay, rather, the favor of God Himself seems to incline more toward the unfortunate as a class; for Jesus Christ calls the poor blessed, and He invites most lovingly all who are in labor or sorrow to come to Him for solace, embracing with special love the lowly and those harassed by injustice. At the realization of these things, the proud spirit of the rich is easily brought down, and the downcast heart of the afflicted is lifted up; the former are moved toward kindness, the latter toward reasonableness in their demands. Thus the distance between the classes, which pride seeks, is seduced, and it will easily be brought to pass that the two classes, with hands clasped in friendship, will be united in heart.

(*Rerum Novarum*, nn. 23–24)

290. We should add here that in today's world there are many other forms of poverty. For are there not certain privations or deprivations which deserve this name? The denial or the limitation of human rights—as, for example, the right to religious freedom, the right to share in the building of society, the freedom to organize and to form unions, or to take initiatives in economic matters—do these not impoverish the human person as much as, if not more than, the deprivation of material goods? And is development which does not take into account the full affirmation of these rights really development on the human level?

(*Sollicitudo Rei Socialis*, n. 15)

291. The fact is that many people, perhaps the majority today, do not have the means which would enable them to take their place in an effective and humanly dignified way within a productive system in which work is truly central.... Thus, if not actually exploited, they are to a great extent marginalized: economic development takes place over their heads, so to speak, when it does not actually reduce the already narrow scope of their old subsistence economies.... Many other people, while not completely marginalized, live in situations in which the struggle for a bare minimum is uppermost.... Unfortunately, the great majority of people in the Third World still live in such conditions.
(*Centesimus Annus*, n. 33)

II. SOCIAL JUSTICE

292. In reality, besides commutative justice, there is also social justice with its own set obligations, from which neither employers nor working men can escape. Now it is of the very essence of social justice to demand from each individual all that is necessary for the common good.
(*Divini Redemptoris*, n. 51)

293. To satisfy the demands of justice and equity, strenuous efforts must be made, without disregarding the rights of persons or the natural qualities of each country, to remove as quickly as possible the immense economic inequalities, which now exist and in many cases are growing and which are connected with individual and social discrimination. Justice and equity likewise require that the mobility, which is necessary in a developing economy, be regulated in such a way as to keep the life of individuals and their families from becoming insecure and precarious. When workers come from

another country or district and contribute to the economic advancement of a nation or region by their labor, all discrimination as regards wages and working conditions must be carefully avoided. All the people, moreover, above all, the public authorities, must treat them not as mere tools of production but as persons, and must help them to bring their families to live with them and to provide themselves with a decent dwelling; they must also see to it that these workers are incorporated into the social life of the country or region that receives them. Employment opportunities, however, should be created in their own areas as far as possible. In economic affairs, which today are subject to change, as in the new forms of industrial society in which automation, for example, is advancing, care must be taken that sufficient and suitable work and the possibility of the appropriate technical and professional formation are furnished. The livelihood and the human dignity, especially of those who are in very difficult conditions because of illness or old age, must be guaranteed.
(*Gaudium et Spes*, n. 66)

294. All of you who have heard the cry of the needy and are trying to meet their needs are the persons we consider the promoters, and, so to speak, the apostles of beneficial and genuine development which, far from consisting in wealth which looks to individual advantage or is sought for its own sake, is rather to be found in an economy adjusted to the welfare of the human person and in daily sustenance provided for all, the source, as it were, of fraternal charity and a clear sign of the help of Divine Providence.
(*Populorum Progressio,* n. 86)

295. Justice is, at one and the same time, a moral virtue and a legal concept. Sometimes it is represented as a blindfolded figure; in effect, though, it is the proper task of justice to be clear-sighted and vigilant in ensuring the balance between rights and duties, in foster-

ing an equitable sharing of burdens and benefits. Justice makes whole; it does not destroy; it leads to reconciliation, not to revenge. Upon examination, at its deepest level, it is rooted in love, which finds its most significant expression in mercy. Therefore, justice, if separated from merciful love, becomes cold and cutting.
(*World Day of Peace Message*, 1998, n. 1)

296. But, as we have often stated, the most important duty in the realm of justice is to allow each country to promote its own development, within the framework of a cooperation free from any spirit of domination, whether economic or political. The complexity of the problems raised is certainly great, in the present intertwining of mutual dependencies. Thus it is necessary to have the courage to undertake a revision of the relationships between nations, whether it is a question of the international division of production, the structure of exchanges, the control of profits, the monetary system—without forgetting the actions of human solidarity—to question the models of growth of the rich nations and change people's outlooks, so that they may realize the prior call of international duty, and to renew international organizations so that they may increase in effectiveness.
(*Octogesima Adveniens*, n. 43)

297. *True mercy is, so to speak, the most profound source of justice.* If justice is in itself suitable for arbitration between people concerning the reciprocal distribution of objective goods in an equitable manner, love and only love (including that kindly love we call mercy) is capable of restoring man to himself.

Mercy that is truly Christian is also, in a certain sense, the most perfect incarnation of equality between people and therefore also the most perfect incarnation of justice as well, insofar as justice aims at the same result in its own sphere. However, the equality brought by justice is limited to the realm of objective and extrinsic goods, while

love and mercy bring it about that people meet one another in that value which is man himself, with the dignity that is proper to him. At the same time, "equality" of people through "patient and kind" love does not take away differences....
(*Dives in Misericordia*, n. 14)

298. All experts in social problems are seeking eagerly a structure so fashioned in accordance with the norms of reason that it can lead economic life back to sound and right order. But this order, which We Ourselves ardently long for and with all Our efforts promote, will be wholly defective and incomplete unless all the activities of men harmoniously unite to imitate and attain, in so far as it lies within human strength, the marvelous unity of the Divine plan. We mean that perfect order which the Church, with great force and power, preaches, and which right human reason itself demands, that all things be directed to God as the first and supreme end of all created activity, and that all created good under God be considered as mere instruments to be used only in so far as they conduce to the attainment of the supreme end. Nor is it to be thought that gainful occupations are thereby belittled or judged less consonant with human dignity; on the contrary, we are taught to recognize in them with reverence the manifest will of the Divine Creator Who placed man upon the earth to work it and use it in a multitude of ways for his needs. Those who are engaged in producing goods, therefore, are not forbidden to increase their fortune in a just and lawful manner; for it is only fair that he who renders service to the community and makes it richer should also, through the increased wealth of the community, be made richer himself according to his position, provided that all these things be sought with due respect for the laws of God and without impairing the rights of others, and that they be employed in accordance with faith and right reason. If these principles are observed by everyone, everywhere, and always, not only the production and acquisition of

goods but also the use of wealth, which now is seen to be so often contrary to right order, will be brought back soon within the bounds of equity and just distribution. The sordid love of wealth, which is the shame and great sin of our age, will be opposed in actual fact by the gentle yet effective law of Christian moderation which commands man to seek first the Kingdom of God and His justice, with the assurance that, by virtue of God's kindness and unfailing promise, temporal goods also, in so far as he has need of them, shall be given him besides.

(*Quadragesimo Anno*, n. 136)

299. Our contemporaries are coming to feel these inequalities with an ever-sharper awareness, since they are thoroughly convinced that the ampler technical and economic possibilities which the world of today enjoys can and should correct this unhappy state of affairs. Hence, many reforms in the socioeconomic realm and a change of mentality and attitude are required of all. For this reason, the Church down through the centuries and in the light of the Gospel has worked out the principles of justice and equity demanded by right reason both for individual and social life and for international life, and she has proclaimed them especially in recent times. This sacred council intends to strengthen these principles according to the circumstances of this age and to set forth certain guidelines, especially with regard to the requirements of economic development.

(*Gaudium et Spes*, n. 63)

III. CHARITY AND THE PREFERENTIAL OPTION FOR THE POOR

300. Charity is the greatest social commandment. It respects others and their rights. It requires the practice of justice, and it alone

makes us capable of it. Charity inspires a life of self-giving: "Whoever seeks to gain his life will lose it, but whoever loses his life will preserve it" (Lk 17:33).
(CCC, n. 1889)

301. It will not be superfluous therefore to reexamine and further clarify in this light the characteristic themes and guidelines dealt with by the Magisterium in the recent years. Here I would like to indicate one of them: the preferential option or love of preference for the poor. This is an option, a special form of primacy in the exercise of Christian charity, to which the whole tradition of the Church bears witness. It affects the life of each Christian inasmuch as he or she seeks to imitate the life of Christ, but it applies equally to our social responsibilities and hence to our manner of living, and to the logical decisions to be made concerning our ownership and the use of goods.
(*Sollicitudo Rei Socialis*, n. 42)

302. Rereading the encyclical [*Rerum Novarum*] in the light of contemporary realities enables us to appreciate the Church's constant concern for and dedication to categories of people who are especially beloved to the Lord Jesus. The content of the text is an excellent testimony to the continuity within the Church of the so-called "preferential option for the poor," an option which I defined as a "special form of primacy in the exercise of Christian charity" (SRS, n. 42).
(*Centesimus Annus*, n. 11)

303. In seeking to promote human dignity, the Church shows a preferential love of the poor and voiceless, because the Lord has identified himself with them in special way (cf. Mt 25:40). This love excludes no one, but simply embodies a priority of service to which the whole Christian tradition bears witness. This love of preference

for the poor, and the decisions which it inspires in us, cannot but embrace the immense multitudes of the hungry, the needy, the homeless, those without medical care and, above all, those without hope of a better future.
(*Ecclesia in Asia*, n. 34)

304. The Church's love of preference for the poor is wonderfully inscribed in Mary's Magnificat. The God of the Covenant, celebrated in the exultation of her spirit by the Virgin of Nazareth, is also he who "has cast down the mighty from their thrones, and lifted up the lowly ... filled the hungry with good things, sent the rich away empty ... scattered the proud-hearted ... and his mercy is from age to age on those who fear him" (Lk 4:18). Mary is deeply imbued with the spirit of the poor of Yahweh, who in the prayer of the Psalms awaited from God their salvation, placing all their trust in him (cf. Ps 25; 31; 35; 55).
(*Redemptoris Mater*, n. 37)

305. "If a brother or a sister be naked," says Saint James, "if they lack their daily nourishment, and one of you says to them:'Go in peace, be warmed and be filled,' without giving them what is necessary for the body, what good does it do?" (Jas 2:15–16) Today no one can be ignorant any longer of the fact that in whole continents countless men and women are ravished by hunger, countless numbers of children are undernourished, so that many of them die in infancy, while the physical growth and mental development of many others are retarded and, as a result, whole regions are condemned to the most depressing despondency.
(*Populorum Progressio*, n. 45)

306. And yet many today go so far as to condemn the Church as the ancient pagans once did, for such outstanding charity, and would

substitute in lieu thereof a system of benevolence established by the laws of the State. But no human devices can ever be found to supplant Christian charity, which gives itself entirely for the benefit of others. This virtue belongs to the Church alone, for, unless it is derived from the Most Sacred Heart of Jesus, it is in no wise a virtue; and whosoever departs from the Church wanders far from Christ. (*Rerum Novarum*, n. 30)

307. As can be readily deduced, and as the Church has always seriously warned, it is proper that the duty of helping the poor and unfortunate should especially stir Catholics, since they are members of the Mystical Body of Christ. "In this we have come to know the love of God," said John the Apostle, "that He laid down His life for us, and we likewise ought to lay down our life for the brethren. He who has the goods of this world and sees his brother in need and closes his heart to him, how does the love of God abide in him?" (1 Jn 3:16–17)
(*Mater et Magistra*, n. 159)

IV. THE WELFARE STATE

308. [I]n exceptional circumstances the State can also exercise a substitute function, when sectors or business systems are too weak or are just getting under way, and are not equal to the task at hand. Such supplementary interventions, which are justified by urgent reasons touching the common good, must be as brief as possible, so as to avoid removing permanently from society and business systems the functions which are properly theirs, and so as to avoid enlarging excessively the sphere of State intervention to the detriment of both economic and civil freedom. In recent years the range of such intervention has vastly expanded, to the point of creating a new type of

state, the so-called 'Welfare State.' This has happened in some countries in order to respond better to many needs and demands, by remedying forms of poverty and deprivation unworthy of the human person. However, excesses and abuses, especially in recent years, have provoked very harsh criticisms of the Welfare State, dubbed the 'Social Assistance State.' Malfunctions and defects in the Social Assistance State are the result of an inadequate understanding of the tasks proper to the State. Here again the principle of subsidiarity must be respected: a community of a higher order should not interfere in the internal life of a community of a lower order, depriving the latter of its functions, but rather should support it in case of need and help to coordinate its activity with the activities of the rest of society, always with a view to the common good. By intervening directly and depriving society of its responsibility, the Social Assistance State leads to a loss of human energies and an inordinate increase of public agencies, which are dominated more by bureaucratic ways of thinking than by concern for serving their clients, and which are accompanied by an enormous increase in spending. In fact, it would appear that needs are best understood and satisfied by people who are closest to them and who act as neighbors to those in need. It should be added that certain kinds of demands often call for a response which is not simply material but which is capable of perceiving the deeper human need. One thinks of the condition of refugees, immigrants, the elderly, the sick, and all those in circumstances which call for assistance, such as drug abusers: all these people can be helped effectively only by those who offer them genuine fraternal support, in addition to the necessary care.
(*Centesimus Annus,* n. 48)

309. If Pope Leo XIII calls upon the State to remedy the condition of the poor in accordance with justice, he does so because of his timely awareness that the state has the duty of watching over the

common good and of ensuring that every sector of social life, not excluding the economic one, contributes to achieving that good, while respecting the rightful autonomy of each sector. This should not, however, lead us to think that Pope Leo expected the state to solve every soci al problem. On the contrary, he frequently insists on necessary limits to the State's intervention and on its instrumental character, inasmuch as the State exists in order to protect their rights and not stifle them.
(*Centesimus Annus*, n. 11)

310. It is not right, as We have said, for either the citizen or the family to be absorbed by the State; it is proper that the individual and the family should be permitted to retain their freedom of action, as far as this is possible without jeopardizing the common good and without injuring anyone. Nevertheless, those who govern must see to it that they protect the community and its constituent parts: the community, because nature has entrusted its safeguarding to the sovereign power in the State to such an extent that the protection of the public welfare is not only the supreme law, but is the entire reason and cause for sovereignty.
(*Rerum Novarum*, n. 35)

ARTICLE NINE

THE ENVIRONMENT

I. THE GOODNESS OF THE CREATED ORDER

311. "And God saw that it was good" (Gn 1:25). These words from the first chapter of the Book of Genesis reveal the meaning of what God has done. To men and women, the crown of the entire process of creation, the Creator entrusts the care of the earth (cf. Gn 2:15). This brings concrete obligations in the area of ecology for every person. Fulfillment of these obligations supposes an openness to a spiritual and ethical perspective capable of overcoming selfish attitudes and lifestyles which lead to the depletion of natural resources. (*Ecclesia in America*, n. 25)

312. The seventh commandment enjoins respect for the integrity of creation. Animals, like plants and inanimate beings, are by nature destined for the common good of past, present, and future humanity. Use of the mineral, vegetable, and animal resources of the universe cannot be divorced from respect for moral imperatives. Man's dominion over inanimate and other living beings granted by the Creator is not absolute; it is limited by concern for the quality of life of his neighbor, including generations to come; it requires a religious respect for the integrity of creation.
(CCC, n. 2415)

II. ENVIRONMENTAL PROBLEMS

313. Everyone certainly knows that in some parts of the world there is an imbalance between the amount of arable land and the size of the population, and, in other parts, between the fertility of the soil and available farm implements. Consequently, necessity demands a cooperative effort on the part of the people to bring about a quicker exchange of goods, or of capital, or the migration of people themselves. (*Pacem in Terris*, n. 101)

314. [N]atural resources are limited; some are not, as it is said, renewable. Using them as if they were inexhaustible, with absolute dominion, seriously endangers their availability not only for the present generation but, above all, for generations to come.... We all know that the direct or indirect result of industrialization is, ever more frequently, the pollution of the environment, with serious consequences for the health of the population. Once again it is evident that development, the planning which governs it, and the way in which resources are used must include respect for moral demands. One of the latter undoubtedly imposes limits on the use of the natural world. The dominion granted to man by the Creator is not an absolute power, nor can one speak of a freedom to 'use and misuse,' or to dispose of things as one pleases. The limitation imposed from the beginning by the Creator himself and expressed symbolically by the prohibition not to "eat of the fruit of the tree" (cf. Gn 2:16–17) shows clearly enough that, when it comes to the natural world, we are subject not only to biological laws but also to moral ones, which cannot be violated with impunity.
(*Sollicitudo Rei Socialis*, n. 34)

315. We seem to be increasingly aware of the fact that the exploitation of the earth, the planet on which we are living, demands rational and honest planning. At the same time, exploitation of the earth not only for industrial but also for military purposes and the uncontrolled development of technology outside the framework of a long-term authentically humanistic plan often bring with them a threat to man's natural environment, alienate him in his relations with nature and remove him from nature.
(*Redemptor Hominis*, n. 15)

316. Equally worrying is the ecological question which accompanies the problem of consumerism and which is closely connected

to it. In his desire to have and to enjoy rather than to be and to grow, man consumes the resources of the earth and his own life in an excessive and disordered way. At the root of the senseless destruction of the natural environment lies an anthropological error, which unfortunately is widespread in our day. Man, who discovers his capacity to transform and, in a certain sense, create the world through his own work, forgets that this is always based on God's prior and original gift of the things that are. Man thinks that he can take arbitrary use of the earth, subjecting it without restraint to his will, as though the earth did not have its own requisites and a prior God-given purpose, which man can indeed develop but must not betray. Instead of carrying out his role as a cooperator with God in the work of creation, man sets himself up in place of God and thus ends up provoking a rebellion on the part of nature, which is more tyrannized than governed by him. In all this, one notes first the poverty or narrowness of man's outlook, motivated as he is by a desire to possess things rather than to relate them to the truth, and lacking that disinterested, unselfish and aesthetic attitude that is born of wonder in the presence of being and of the beauty which enables one to see in visible things the message of the invisible God who created them. In this regard, humanity today must be conscious of its duties and obligations towards future generations.

(*Centesimus Annus,* n. 37)

317. While the horizon of man is thus being modified according to the images that are chosen for him, another transformation is making itself felt, one which is the dramatic and unexpected consequence of human activity. Man is suddenly becoming aware that by an ill-considered exploitation of nature he risks destroying it and becoming, in his turn, the victim of this degradation. Not only is the material environment becoming a permanent menace—pollution and refuse, new illness and absolute destructive capacity—but the human

framework is no longer under man's control, thus creating an environment for tomorrow which may well be intolerable. This is a wide-ranging social problem which concerns the entire human family. The Christian must turn to these new perceptions in order to take on responsibility, together with the rest of men, for a destiny which from now on is shared by all.
(*Octogesima Adveniens*, n. 21)

318. In addition to the irrational destruction of the natural environment, we must also mention the more serious destruction of the *human environment,* something which is by no means receiving the attention it deserves. Although people are rightly worried—though much less than they should be—about preserving the natural habitats of the various animal species threatened with extinction, because they realize that each of these species makes its particular contribution to the balance of nature in general, too little effort is made to *safeguard the moral conditions for an authentic 'human ecology.'* Not only has God given the earth to man, who must use it with respect for the original good purpose for which it was given to him, but man, too, is God's gift to man. He must therefore respect the natural and moral structure with which he has been endowed. In this context, mention should be made of the serious problems of modern urbanization, of the need for urban planning which is concerned with how people are to live, and of the attention which should be given to a 'social ecology' of work.
(*Centesimus Annus*, n. 38)

III. Environmental Stewardship

319. As one called to till and look after the garden of the world (cf. Gn 2:15), man has a specific responsibility towards the environ-

ment in which he lives, towards the creation which God has put at the service of his personal dignity, of his life, not only for the present but also for future generations. It is the ecological question—ranging from the preservation of the natural habitats of the different species of animals and of other forms of life to 'human ecology' properly speaking—which finds in the Bible clear and strong ethical direction, leading to a solution which respects the great good of life, of every life. In fact, "the dominion granted to man by the Creator is not an absolute power, nor can one speak of a freedom to 'use and misuse,' or to dispose of things as one pleases. The limitation imposed from the beginning by the Creator himself and expressed symbolically by the prohibition not to 'eat of the fruit of the tree' (cf. Gn 2:16–17) shows clearly enough that, when it comes to the natural world, we are subject not only to biological laws but also to moral ones, which cannot be violated with impunity" (SRS, n. 34).
(*Evangelium Vitae*, n. 42)

320. Those responsible for business enterprises are responsible to society for the economic and ecological effects of their operations. They have an obligation to consider the good of persons and not only the increase of profits. Profits are necessary, however. They make possible the investments that ensure the future of a business, and they guarantee employment.
(CCC, n. 2432)

321. The promotion of human dignity is linked to the right to a healthy environment, since this right highlights the dynamics of the relationship between the individual and the society. A body of international, regional, and national norms on the environment is gradually giving juridic form to this right. But juridic measures are by themselves not sufficient.... The world's present and future depend on the safeguarding of creation, because of the endless interdependence

between human beings and their environment. Placing human well-being at the center of concern for the environment is actually the surest way of safeguarding creation.
(*World Day of Peace Message*, 1999, n. 10)

IV. TECHNOLOGY

322. The development of industry and of the various sectors connected with it, even the most modern electronics technology, especially in the fields of miniaturization, communications and telecommunications and so forth, shows how vast is the role of technology, that ally of work that human thought has produced, in the interaction between the subject and the object of work (in the widest sense of the word).... [T]echnology is undoubtedly man's ally. It facilitates his work, perfects, accelerates and augments it. However, it is also a fact that, in some instances, technology can cease to be man's ally and become almost his enemy, as when the mechanization of work supplants him, taking away all personal satisfaction and the incentive to creativity and responsibility, when it deprives many workers of their employment, or when through exalting the machine, it reduces man to the status of its slave.
(*Laborem Exercens*, n. 5)

323. The present generation knows that it is in a privileged position: progress provides it with countless possibilities that only a few decades ago were undreamed of. Man's creative activity, his intelligence and his work, have brought about profound changes both in the field of science and technology and in that of social and cultural life. Man has extended power over nature and has acquired deeper knowledge of the laws of social behavior.... Today's young people, especially, know that the progress of science and technology

can produce not only new material goods but also a wider sharing in knowledge.... The achievements of biological, psychological and social science will help man to understand better the riches of his own being.... But side by side with all this, or rather, as part of it, there are also difficulties that appear whenever there is growth.
(*Dives in Misericordia*, n. 10)

ARTICLE TEN

THE INTERNATIONAL
COMMUNITY

I. THE HUMAN FAMILY

324. According to biblical Revelation, God created the human being—man and woman—in his image and likeness. This bond between the human person and the Creator provides the basis of his or her dignity and fundamental inalienable rights, of which God is the guarantor. To these personal rights obviously correspond duties toward others. Neither the individual nor society, the State nor any human institution can reduce a person, or a group of persons, to the status of an object. Revelation, indeed, insists just as much on the unity of the human family: all persons created in God have the same origin. Whatever throughout history may have been their dispersion or the accentuation of their differences, they are destined to form one sole family according to God's plan established 'in the beginning.' As St. Paul told the Athenians: "From one single stock he created the whole human race so that they could occupy the entire earth," and so everyone can say with the poet that they are of God's same 'race.' (*The Church and Racism*, nn. 19–20)

325. Moreover, the Church by divine right pertains to all nations. This is confirmed by the fact that she already is everywhere on earth and strives to embrace all peoples.
(*Mater et Magistra*, n. 178)

326. At that point, awareness of the common fatherhood of God, of the brotherhood of all in Christ—children in the Son—and of the presence and life-giving action of the Holy Spirit will bring our vision of the world a new criterion for interpreting it. Beyond human and natural bonds, already so close and strong, there is discerned in the light of faith a new model of the unity of the human race, which must ultimately inspire our solidarity.
(*Sollicitudo Rei Socialis*, n. 40)

II. FREE TRADE

327. The teaching of Leo XIII in *Rerum Novarum* is always valid: if the positions of the contracting parties are too unequal, the consent of the parties does not suffice to guarantee the justice of their contract, and the rule of free agreement remains subservient to the demands of the natural law. What was true of the just wage for the individual is also true of international contracts: an economy of exchange can no longer be based solely on the law of free competition, a law which, in its turn, too often creates an economic dictatorship. Freedom of trade is fair only if it is subject to the demands of social justice.
(*Populorum Progressio,* n. 59)

328. There is a need to establish a greater justice in the sharing of goods, both within national communities and on the international level. In international exchanges there is a need to go beyond relationships based on force, in order to arrive at agreements reached with the good of all in mind. Relationships based on force have never, in fact, established justice in a true and lasting manner, even if at certain times the alteration of positions can often make it possible to find easier conditions for dialogue. The use of force, moreover, leads to the setting in motion of opposing forces, and from this, springs a climate of struggle which opens the way to situations of extreme violence and to abuses. But, as we have often stated, the most important duty in the realm of justice is to allow each country to promote its own development, within the framework of a cooperation free from any spirit of domination, whether economic or political. The complexity of the problems raised is certainly great, in the present intertwining of mutual dependencies. Thus it is necessary to have the courage to undertake a revision of the relationships between nations, whether it is a question of the international division of production,

the structure of exchanges, the control of profits, the monetary system—without forgetting the actions of human solidarity—to question the models of growth of the rich nations and change people's outlooks, so that they may realize the prior call of international duty, and to renew international organizations so that they may increase in effectiveness.

(*Octogesima Adveniens*, n. 43)

329. In this area one cannot employ two systems of weights and measures. What holds for a national economy or among developed countries is valid also in commercial relations between rich nations and poor nations. Without abolishing the competitive market, it should be kept within the limits which make it just and moral, and therefore human. In trade between developed and underdeveloped economies, conditions are too disparate, and the degrees of genuine freedom available too unequal. In order that international trade be human and moral, social justice requires that it restore to the participants a certain equality of opportunity. This equality is a long-term objective, but to reach it, we must begin now to create true equality in discussions and negotiations. Here again, international agreements on a rather wide scale would be helpful: they would establish general norms for regulating certain prices, for guaranteeing certain types of production, for supporting certain new industries. Who is there who does not see that such a common effort aimed at increased justice in business relations between peoples would bestow on developing nations positive assistance, the effects of which would be not only immediate but lasting?

(*Populorum Progressio*, n. 61)

179

III. PEACE AND WAR

330. Peace is not merely the absence of war; nor can it be reduced solely to the maintenance of a balance of power between
enemies; nor is it brought about by dictatorship. Instead, it is rightly
and appropriately called an enterprise of justice. Peace results from
that order structured into human society by its divine Founder, and
actualized by men as they thirst after ever greater justice. The common good of humanity finds its ultimate meaning in the eternal law.
But since the concrete demands of this common good are constantly
changing as time goes on, peace is never attained once and for all,
but must be built up ceaselessly. Moreover, since the human will is
unsteady and wounded by sin, the achievement of peace requires a
constant mastering of passions and the vigilance of lawful authority.
But this is not enough. This peace on earth cannot be obtained unless
personal well-being is safeguarded and men freely and trustingly share
with one another the riches of their inner spirits and their talents. A
firm determination to respect other men and peoples and their dignity, as well as the studied practice of brotherhood, are absolutely
necessary for the establishment of peace. Hence, peace is likewise
the fruit of love, which goes beyond what justice can provide. That
earthly peace which arises from love of neighbor symbolizes and
results from the peace of Christ which radiates from God the Father.
For by the cross the incarnate Son, the prince of peace reconciled all
men with God. By thus restoring all men to the unity of one people
and one body, He slew hatred in His own flesh; and, after being lifted
on high by His resurrection, He poured forth the spirit of love into
the hearts of men. For this reason, all Christians are urgently summoned to do in love what the truth requires, and to join with all true
peacemakers in pleading for peace and bringing it about. Motivated
by this same spirit, we cannot fail to praise those who renounce the
use of violence in the vindication of their rights and who resort to

methods of defense which are otherwise available to weaker parties, too, provided this can be done without injury to the rights and duties of others or of the community itself.
(*Gaudium et Spes*, n. 78)

331. Respect for and development of human life require peace. Peace is not merely the absence of war, and it is not limited to maintaining a balance of powers between adversaries. Peace cannot be attained on earth without safeguarding the goods of persons, free communication among men, respect for the dignity of persons and peoples, and the assiduous practice of fraternity. Peace is "the tranquillity of order" (St. Augustine, *De civ. Dei*, IX.13.1). Peace is the work of justice and the effect of charity.
(CCC, n. 2304)

332. Injustice, excessive economic or social inequalities, envy, distrust, and pride raging among men and nations constantly threaten peace and cause wars. Everything done to overcome these disorders contributes to building up peace and avoiding war: "Insofar as men are sinners, the threat of war hangs over them and will so continue until Christ comes again; but insofar as they can vanquish sin by coming together in charity, violence itself will be vanquished and these words will be fulfilled: 'they shall beat their swords into plowshares, and their spears into pruning hooks; nation shall not lift up sword against nation, neither shall they learn war anymore'" (GS, n. 78; cf. Is 2:4).
(CCC, n. 2317)

333. Non-combatants, wounded soldiers, and prisoners must be respected and treated humanely. Actions deliberately contrary to the law of nations and to its universal principles are crimes, as are the orders that command such actions. Blind obedience does not suffice

to excuse those who carry them out. Thus the extermination of a people, nation, or ethnic minority must be condemned as a mortal sin. One is morally bound to resist orders that command genocide. (CCC, n. 2313)

IV. ARMS

334. On the other hand, it is with deep sorrow that We note the enormous stocks of armaments that have been and still are being made in more economically developed countries, with a vast outlay of intellectual and economic resources. And so it happens that, while the people of these countries are loaded with heavy burdens, other countries, as a result, are deprived of the collaboration they need in order to make economic and social progress.
(*Pacem in Terris*, n. 109)

335. "I was hungry and you gave me no food ... naked and you did not clothe me ... in prison and you did not visit me" (Mt 25:42). These words become charged with even stronger warning, when we think that, instead of bread and cultural aid, the new States and nations awakening to independent life are being offered,sometimes in abundance, modern weapons and means of destruction placed at the service of armed conflicts and wars that are not so much a requirement for defending their just rights and their sovereignty, but rather a form of chauvinism, imperialism, and neocolonialism of one kind or another.
(*Redemptor Hominis*, n. 16)

336. The teaching of the Catholic Church in this area has been clear and consistent. It has deplored the arms race, called nonetheless for mutual progressive and verifiable reduction of armaments as well

as greater safeguards against possible misuse of these weapons. It has done so while urging that the independence, freedom, and legitimate security of each and every nation be respected. (*Message to the Second Special Session of the United Nations for Disarmament,* n. 5)

337. An insane arms race swallowed up the resources needed for the development of national economies and for assistance to the less developed nations. Scientific and technological progress, which should have contributed to man's well-being, was transformed into an instrument of war: science and technology were directed to the production of ever more efficient and destructive weapons. (*Centesimus Annus,* n. 18)

V. THE UNIVERSAL COMMON GOOD

338. Human interdependence is increasing and gradually spreading throughout the world. The unity of the human family, embracing people who enjoy equal natural dignity, implies a universal common good. This good calls for an organization of the community of nations able to "provide for the different needs of men; this will involve the sphere of social life to which belong questions of food, hygiene, education ... and certain situations arising here and there, as for example ... alleviating the miseries of refugees dispersed throughout the world, and assisting migrants and their families" (GS, n. 84). (CCC, n. 1911)

339. Like the common good of individual states, so too the universal common good cannot be determined except by having regard for the human person. Therefore, the public and universal authority, too, must have as its fundamental objective the recognition, respect,

safeguarding and promotion of the rights of the human person; this can be done by direct action when required, or by creating on a world scale an environment in which leaders of the individual countries can suitably maintain their own functions.
(*Pacem in Terris*, n. 139)

VI. TRANSNATIONAL AND INTERNATIONAL ORGANIZATIONS

340. It is therefore our ardent desire that the United Nations Organization in its structure and in its means may become ever more equal to the magnitude and nobility of its tasks, and may the time come as quickly as possible when every human being will find therein an effective safeguard for the rights which derive directly from his dignity as a person, and which are therefore universal, inviolable, and inalienable rights. This is all the more to be hoped for since all human beings, as they take an ever more active part in the public life of their own country, are showing an increasing interest in the affairs of all peoples, and are becoming more consciously aware that they are living members of the whole human family.
(*Pacem in Terris*, n. 145)

341. [I]nternational collaboration on a worldwide scale requires institutions that will prepare, coordinate and direct it, until finally there is established an order of justice which is universally recognized. With all Our heart, We encourage these organizations which have undertaken this collaboration for the development of the peoples of the world, and Our wish is that they grow in prestige and authority. "Your vocation," as We said to the representatives of the United Nations in New York, "is to bring not some people but all peoples to treat each other as brothers...."
(*Populorum Progressio*, n. 78)

342. Since the relationships between countries today are closer in every region of the world, by reason of science and technology, it is proper that peoples become more and more interdependent. Accordingly, contemporary problems of the moment—whether in the fields of science and technology, or of economic and social affairs, or of public administration, or of cultural advancement—these, because they may exceed the capacities of individual States, very often affect a number of nations and, at times, all the nations of the earth.

As a result, individual countries, although advanced in culture and civilization, in number and industry of citizens, in wealth, in geographical extent, are not able by themselves to resolve satisfactorily their basic problems. Accordingly, because States must on occasion complement or perfect one another, they really consult their own interests only when they take into account at the same time the interests of others. Hence, dire necessity warns commonwealths to cooperate among themselves and provide mutual assistance.
(*Mater et Magistra*, nn. 200–202)

343. But it is necessary to go still further. At Bombay, We called for the establishment of a great World Fund, to be made up of part of the money spent on arms, to relieve the most destitute of this world (Paul VI, *Message to the World, Entrusted to Journalists*). What is true of the immediate struggle against want, holds good also when there is a question of development. Only worldwide collaboration, of which a common fund would be both means and symbol, will succeed in overcoming vain rivalries and in establishing a fruitful and peaceful exchange between peoples.
(*Populorum Progressio*, n. 51)

VII. IMMIGRATION

344. The sentiment of universal fatherhood which the Lord has placed in Our heart makes Us feel profound sadness in considering the phenomenon of political refugees: a phenomenon which has assumed large proportions and which always hides numberless and acute sufferings.

Such expatriations show that there are some political regimes which do not guarantee for individual citizens a sufficient sphere of freedom within which their souls are allowed to breathe humanly; in fact, under those regimes even the lawful existence of such a sphere of freedom is either called into question or denied. This undoubtedly is a radical inversion of the order of human society, because the reason for the existence of public authority is to promote the common good, a fundamental element of which is the recognition of that sphere of freedom and the safeguarding of it.

(*Pacem in Terris*, nn. 103–104)

345. In its history, America has experienced many immigrations, as waves of men and women came to its various regions in the hope of a better future. The phenomenon continues even today, especially with many people and families from Latin American countries who have moved to the northern parts of the continent, to the point where, in some cases, they constitute a substantial part of the population. They often bring with them a cultural and religious heritage which is rich in Christian elements. The Church is well aware of the problems created by this situation and is committed to spare no effort in developing her own pastoral strategy among these immigrant people, in order to help them settle in their new land and to foster a welcoming attitude among the local population, in the belief that a mutual openness will bring enrichment to all. Church communities will not fail to see in this phenomenon a specific call to live an evangelical frater-

nity and at the same time a summons to strengthen their own religious spirit with a view to a more penetrating evangelization. With this in mind, the Synod Fathers recalled that the Church in America must be a vigilant advocate, defending against any unjust restriction the natural right of individual persons to move freely within their own nation and from one nation to another. Attention must be called to the rights of migrants and their families, and to respect for their human dignity, even in cases of non-legal immigration. Migrants should be met with a hospitable and welcoming attitude which can encourage them to become part of the Church's life, always with due regard for their freedom and their specific cultural identity. Cooperation between the dioceses from which they come and those in which they settle, also through specific pastoral structures provided for in the legislation and praxis of the Church, has proved extremely beneficial to this end. In this way, the most adequate and complete pastoral care possible can be ensured. The Church in America must be constantly concerned to provide for the effective evangelization of those recent arrivals who do not yet know Christ.

(*Ecclesia in America*, n. 65)

346. From bitter experience, then, we know that the fear of 'difference,' especially when it expresses itself in a narrow and exclusive nationalism which denies any rights to 'the other,' can lead to a true nightmare of violence and terror. And yet if we make the effort to look at matters objectively, we can see that, transcending all the differences which distinguish individuals and peoples, there is a fundamental commonality. For different cultures are but different ways of facing the question of the meaning of personal existence. And it is precisely here that we find one source of the respect which is due to every culture and every nation.

(*Address to the Fiftieth General Assembly of the United Nations Organization*, 1995, n. 9)

VIII. Foreign Debt

347. The existence of a foreign debt which is suffocating quite a few countries of the American continent represents a complex problem. While not entering into its many aspects, the Church, in her pastoral concern, cannot ignore this difficult situation, since it touches the life of so many people. For this reason, different Episcopal Conferences in America, conscious of the gravity of the question, have organized study meetings on the subject and have published documents aimed at pointing out workable solutions. I, too, have frequently expressed my concern about this situation, which in some cases has become unbearable. In light of the imminent Great Jubilee of the Year 2000, and recalling the social significance that Jubilees had in the Old Testament, I wrote: "In the spirit of the Book of Leviticus (25:8–12), Christians will have to raise their voice on behalf of all the poor of the world, proposing the Jubilee as an appropriate time to give thought, among other things, to reducing substantially, if not cancelling outright, the international debt which seriously threatens the future of many nations" (TMA, n. 36).

Once more I express the hope, which the Synod Fathers made their own, that the Pontifical Council for Justice and Peace, together with other competent agencies, such as the Section for Relations with States of the Secretariat of State, through study and dialogue with representatives of the First World and with the leaders of the World Bank and the International Monetary Fund, will seek ways of resolving the problem of the foreign debt and produce guidelines that would prevent similar situations from recurring on the occasion of future loans. On the broadest level possible, it would be helpful if internationally known experts in economics and monetary questions would undertake a critical analysis of the world economic order, in its positive and negative aspects, so as to correct the present order, and that they would propose a system and mechanisms capable of ensuring an integral and concerted development of individuals and peoples. (*Ecclesia in America*, n. 59)

348. Furthermore, in her search for justice in a world marred by social and economic inequalities, the Church cannot ignore the heavy burden incurred by many developing nations in Asia, with its consequent impact upon their present and future. In many cases, these countries are forced to cut down spending on the necessities of life, such as food, health, housing, and education, in order to service their debts to international monetary agencies and banks. This means that people are trapped in living conditions which are an affront to human dignity.
(*Ecclesia in Asia*, n. 40)

349. The Synod Fathers voiced concern about the external debt afflicting many American nations and expressed solidarity with them. They were consistent in reminding public opinion of the complexity of this issue, acknowledging that the debt is often the result of corruption and poor administration. In keeping with the spirit of the Synod's deliberations, such an acknowledgment does not mean to place on one side all the blame for a phenomenon which is extremely complex in its origin and in the solutions which it demands. Among the causes which have helped to create massive external debt are not only high interest rates, caused by speculative financial policies, but also the irresponsibility of people in government who, in incurring debt, have given too little thought to the real possibility of repaying it. This has been aggravated by the fact that huge sums obtained through international loans sometimes go to enrich individuals instead of being used to pay for the changes needed for the country's development. At the same time, it would be unjust to impose the burden resulting from these irresponsible decisions upon those who did not make them. The gravity of the situation is all the more evident

when we consider that even the payment of interest alone represents a burden for the economy of poor nations, which deprives the authorities of the money necessary for social development, education, health and the establishment of a fund to create jobs.
(*Ecclesia in America*, n. 22)

IX. NATIONALISM AND ETHNIC TENSIONS

350. Among still other obstacles which are opposed to the formation of a world which is more just and which is better organized toward a universal solidarity, We wish to speak of nationalism and racism. It is only natural that communities which have recently reached their political independence should be jealous of a national unity which is still fragile, and that they should strive to protect it. Likewise, it is to be expected that nations endowed with an ancient culture should be proud of the patrimony which their history has bequeathed to them. But these legitimate feelings should be ennobled by that universal charity which embraces the entire human family. Nationalism isolates people from their true good. It would be especially harmful where the weakness of national economies demands rather the pooling of efforts, of knowledge and of funds, in order to implement programs of development and to increase commercial and cultural exchange.
(*Populorum Progressio*, n. 62)

351. The first of these principles is the inalienable dignity of every human person, irrespective of racial, ethnic, cultural, or national origin, or religious belief. Individuals do not exist for themselves alone, but achieve their full identity in relation to others. The same can be said about groups of people.
(*World Day of Peace Message*, 1989, n. 3)

352. Even today, much remains to be done to overcome religious intolerance, which in different parts of the world is closely connected with the oppression of minorities. Unfortunately, we are still witnessing attempts to impose a particular religious idea on others, either directly, by proselytism, which relies on means which are truly coercive, or indirectly, by the denial of certain civil or political rights.... Intolerance can also result from the recurring temptation to fundamentalism, which easily leads to serious abuses such as the radical suppression of all public manifestations of diversity, or even the outright denial of freedom of expression. Fundamentalism can also lead to the exclusion of others from civil society.
(*World Day of Peace Message*, 1991, n. 4)

353. Racism is not the exclusive lot of young nations, where sometimes it hides beneath the rivalries of clans and political parties, with heavy losses for justice and at the risk of civil war. During the colonial period, it often flared up between the colonists and the indigenous population, and stood in the way of mutually profitable understanding, often giving rise to bitterness in the wake of genuine injustices. It is still an obstacle to collaboration among disadvantaged nations and a cause of division and hatred within countries whenever individuals and families see the inviolable rights of the human person held in scorn, as they themselves are unjustly subjected to a regime of discrimination because of their race or their color.
(*Populorum Progressio,* n. 63)

354. If the Church in America, in fidelity to the Gospel of Christ, intends to walk the path of solidarity, she must devote special attention to those ethnic groups which even today experience discrimination. Every attempt to marginalize the indigenous peoples must be eliminated. This means, first of all, respecting their territories

191

and the pacts made with them; likewise, efforts must be made to satisfy their legitimate social, health and cultural requirements. And how can we overlook the need for reconciliation between the indigenous peoples and the societies in which they are living?
(*Ecclesia in America*, n. 64)

355. Racism and racist acts must be condemned. The application of legislative, disciplinary and administrative measures, or even appropriate external pressure, can be timely. Countries and international organizations have at their disposal a whole range of initiatives to be taken or encouraged. It is equally the responsibility of the citizens concerned, but without, for that reason, going so far as to replace violently one unjust situation with another injustice. Constructive solutions must always be envisaged.
(*The Church and Racism*, n. 33)

356. Lay people, whose particular vocation places them in the midst of the world and in charge of the most varied temporal tasks, must for this very reason exercise a very special form of evangelization.... Their own field of evangelizing activity is the vast and complicated world of politics, society and economics, but also the world of culture, of the sciences and the arts, of international life, of the mass media. It also includes other realities which are open to evangelization, such as human love, the family, the education of children and adolescents, professional work, suffering.
(*Evangelii Nuntiandi*, n. 70)

X. THE GLOBAL ECONOMY

357. A feature of the contemporary world is the tendency towards globalization, a phenomenon which, although not exclusively

American, is more obvious and has greater repercussions in America. It is a process made inevitable by increasing communication between the different parts of the world, leading in practice to overcoming distances, with evident effects in widely different fields. The ethical implications can be positive or negative. There is an economic globalization which brings some positive consequences, such as efficiency and increased production and which, with the development of economic links between the different countries, can help to bring greater unity among peoples and make possible a better service to the human family. However, if globalization is ruled merely by the laws of the market applied to suit the powerful, the consequences cannot but be negative. These are, for example, the absolutizing of the economy, unemployment, the reduction and deterioration of public services, the destruction of the environment and natural resources, the growing distance between rich and poor, unfair competition which puts the poor nations in a situation of ever increasing inferiority. While acknowledging the positive values which come with globalization, the Church considers with concern the negative aspects which follow in its wake.
(*Ecclesia in America*, n. 20)

358. If an authentic economic order is to be established on a worldwide basis, an end will have to be put to profiteering, to national ambitions, to the appetite for political supremacy, to militaristic calculations, and to machinations for the sake of spreading and imposing ideologies.
(*Gaudium et Spes*, n. 85)

359. As I mentioned earlier, the complex phenomenon of globalization is one of the features of the contemporary world particularly visible in America. An important part of this many-faceted reality is the economic aspect. By her social doctrine the Church makes an

effective contribution to the issues presented by the current global-ized economy. Her moral vision in this area rests on the threefold cornerstone of human dignity, solidarity and subsidiarity. The glo-balized economy must be analyzed in the light of the principles of social justice, respecting the preferential option for the poor, who must be allowed to take their place in such an economy, and the requirements of the international common good. For the Church's social doctrine is a moral vision which aims to encourage govern-ments, institutions and private organizations to shape a future consonant with the dignity of every person. Within this perspective it is possible to examine questions of external debt, internal political corruption and discrimination both within and between nations. The Church in America is called not only to promote greater integration between nations, thus helping to create an authentic globalized cul-ture of solidarity, but also to cooperate with every legitimate means in reducing the negative effects of globalization, such as the domina-tion of the powerful over the weak, especially in the economic sphere, and the loss of the values of local cultures in favor of a misconstrued homogenization.

(*Ecclesia in America*, n. 55)

360. However much society worldwide shows signs of fragmen-tation, expressed in the conventional names First, Second, Third and even Fourth World, their interdependence remains close. When this interdependence is separated from its ethical requirements, it has di-sastrous consequences for the weakest. Indeed, as a result of a sort of internal dynamic and under the impulse of mechanisms which can only be called perverse, this interdependence triggers negative ef-fects even in the rich countries. It is precisely within these countries that one encounters, though on a lesser scale, the more specific mani-festations of underdevelopment. Thus it should be obvious that development either becomes shared in common by every part of the

world or it undergoes a process of regression even in zones marked by constant progress. This tells us a great deal about the nature of authentic development: either all the nations of the world participate, or it will not be true development.
(*Sollicitudo Rei Socialis*, n. 17)

361. Circumstances have changed, both within the debtor nations and in the international financial market; the instrument chosen to make a contribution to development has turned into a counterproductive mechanism. This is because the debtor nations, in order to service their debt, find themselves obliged to export the capital needed for improving or at least maintaining their standard of living. It is also because, for the same reason, they are unable to obtain new and equally essential financing.
(*Sollicitudo Rei Socialis*, n. 19)

362. Another important area in which the Church is present in every part of America is social and charitable work. The many initiatives on behalf of the elderly, the sick and the needy, through nursing homes, hospitals, dispensaries, canteens providing free meals, and other social centers are a concrete testimony of the preferential love for the poor which the Church in America nurtures. She does so because of her love for the Lord and because she is aware that "Jesus identified himself with the poor" (cf. Mt 25:31–46). In this task which has no limits, the Church in America has been able to create a sense of practical solidarity among the various communities of the continent and of the world, showing in this way the fraternal spirit which must characterize Christians in every time and place.

For this service of the poor to be both evangelical and evangelizing, it must faithfully reflect the attitude of Jesus, who came "to proclaim Good News to the poor" (Lk 4:18). When offered in this spirit, the service of the poor shows forth God's infinite love for

all people and becomes an effective way of communicating the hope of salvation which Christ has brought to the world, a hope which glows in a special way when it is shared with those abandoned or rejected by society. This constant dedication to the poor and disadvantaged emerges in the Church's social teaching, which ceaselessly invites the Christian community to a commitment to overcome every form of exploitation and oppression. It is a question not only of alleviating the most serious and urgent needs through individual actions here and there, but of uncovering the roots of evil and proposing initiatives to make social, political and economic structures more just and fraternal.
(*Ecclesia in America,* n. 18)

363. One of the principal characteristics of our time is the multiplication of social relationships, that is, a daily more complex interdependence of citizens, introducing into their lives and activities many and varied forms of association, recognized for the most part in private and even in public law. This tendency seemingly stems from a number of factors operative in the present era, among which are technical and scientific progress, greater productive efficiency, and a higher standard of living among citizens.
(*Mater et Magistra,* n. 59)

364. Since the relationships between countries today are closer in every region of the world, by reason of science and technology, it is proper that peoples become more and more interdependent. Accordingly, contemporary problems of moment—whether in the fields of science and technology, or of economic and social affairs, or of public administration, or of cultural advancement—these, because they may exceed the capacities of individual States, very often affect a number of nations and, at times, all of the nations of the earth.
(*Mater et Magistra,* nn. 200–201)

ARTICLE ELEVEN

CONCLUSION

I. THE CHALLENGE OF CATHOLIC SOCIAL TEACHING

365. After formulating principles and guidelines for the solution of the worker question, Pope Leo XIII made this incisive statement: "Everyone should put his hand to the work which falls to his share, and that at once and straightway, lest the evil which is already so great become, through delay, absolutely beyond remedy," and he added, "in regard to the Church, her cooperation will never be found lacking" (RN, n. 51).
(*Centesimus Annus*, n. 56)

366. This is the plea, Venerable Brothers, we make at the close of this Letter, to which we have for a considerable time directed our concern about the Universal Church. We desire that the divine Redeemer of mankind, "who has become for us God-given wisdom, and justice, and sanctification, and redemption" (1 Cor 1:30) may reign and triumph gloriously in all things and over all things, for centuries on end. We desire that, in a properly organized order of social affairs, all nations will at last enjoy prosperity, and happiness, and peace.
(*Mater et Magistra*, n. 263)

367. As far as the Church is concerned, the social message of the Gospel must not be considered a theory, but, above all else, a basis and a motivation for action. Inspired by this message, some of the first Christians distributed their goods to the poor, bearing witness to the fact that, despite different social origins, it was possible for people to live together in peace and harmony. Through the power of the Gospel, down the centuries monks tilled the land, men and women Religious founded hospitals and shelters for the poor, confraternities as well as individual men and women of all states of life

devoted themselves to the needy and to those on the margins of society, convinced as they were that Christ's words, "as you did it to one of the least of these my brethren, you did it to me" (Mt 25:40), were not intended to remain a pious wish, but were meant to become a concrete life commitment. Today more than ever, the Church is aware that her social message will gain credibility more immediately from the witness of actions than as a result of its internal logic and consistency. This awareness is also a source of her preferential option for the poor, which is never exclusive or discriminatory towards other groups. This option is not limited to material poverty, since it is well known that there are many other forms of poverty, especially in modern society—not only economic but cultural and spiritual poverty as well. The Church's love for the poor, which is essential for her and a part of her constant tradition, impels her to give attention to a world in which poverty is threatening to assume massive proportions in spite of technological and economic progress. In the countries of the West, different forms of poverty are being experienced by groups which live on the margins of society, by the elderly and the sick, by the victims of consumerism, and even more immediately by so many refugees and migrants. In the developing countries, tragic crises loom on the horizon unless internationally coordinated measures are taken before it is too late.
(*Centesimus Annus*, n. 57)

368. In this commitment, the sons and daughters of the Church must serve as examples and guides, for they are called upon, in conformity with the program announced by Jesus himself in the synagogue at Nazareth, to "preach good news to the poor ... to proclaim release to the captives and recovering of sight to the blind, to set at liberty those who are oppressed, to proclaim the acceptable year of the Lord" (Lk 4:18–19). It is appropriate to emphasize the preeminent role that belongs to the laity, both men and women, as

was reaffirmed in the recent Assembly of the Synod. It is their task to animate temporal realities with Christian commitment, by which they show that they are witnesses and agents of peace and justice. I wish to address especially those who, through the sacrament of Baptism and the profession of the same Creed, share a real, though imperfect, communion with us. I am certain that the concern expressed in this Encyclical, as well as the motives inspiring it, will be familiar to them, for these motives are inspired by the Gospel of Jesus Christ. We can find here a new invitation to bear witness together to our common convictions concerning the dignity of man, created by God, redeemed by Christ, made holy by the Spirit and called upon in this world to live a life in conformity with this dignity. I likewise address this appeal to the Jewish people, who share with us the inheritance of Abraham, "our father in faith" (cf. Rom 4:11) and the tradition of the Old Testament, as well as to the Muslims who, like us, believe in a just and merciful God. And I extend it to all the followers of the world's great religions.
(*Sollicitudo Rei Socialis*, n. 47)

369. It is to all Christians that we address a fresh and insistent call to action. In our encyclical on the Development of Peoples, we urged that all should set themselves to the task: "Laymen should take up as their own proper task the renewal of the temporal order. If the role of the hierarchy is to teach and to interpret authentically the norms of morality to be followed in this matter, it belongs to the laity, without waiting passively for orders and directives, to take the initiatives freely and to infuse a Christian spirit into the mentality, customs, laws and structures of the community in which they live" (PP, n. 42). Let each one examine himself, to see what he has done up to now, and what he ought to do. It is not enough to recall principles, state intentions, point to crying injustice and utter prophetic denunciations; these words will lack real weight unless they are

accompanied for each individual by a livelier awareness of personal responsibility and by effective action. It is too easy to throw back on others responsibility for injustice, if at the same time one does not realize how each one shares in it personally and how personal conversion is needed first. This basic humility will rid action of all inflexibility and sectarianism; it will also avoid discouragement in the face of a task which seems limitless in size. The Christian's hope comes primarily from the fact that he knows that the Lord is working with us in the world, continuing in His Body which is the Church and, through the Church, in the whole of mankind—the Redemption which was accomplished on the cross and which burst forth in victory on the morning of the resurrection. This hope springs also from the fact that the Christian knows that other men are at work, to undertake actions of justice and peace working for the same ends. For beneath an outward appearance of indifference, in the heart of every man there is a will to live in brotherhood and a thirst for justice and peace, which is to be expanded.

(*Octogesima Adveniens*, n. 48)

Catechism of the Catholic Church (1994).

Code of Canon Law (1983).

John XXIII. Encyclical Letter *Mater et Magistra* (On Social Progress), May 15, 1961.

_____. Encyclical Letter *Pacem in Terris* (Peace on Earth), April 11, 1963.

John Paul II. Address at the Third General Conference of the Latin American Bishops, January 28, 1979.

_____. Address to the Fiftieth General Assembly of the United Nations Organization, October 5, 1995.

_____. Address to the Seventh Symposium of European Bishops, 1989.

_____. Apostolic Exhortation *Familiaris Consortio* (The Role of the Christian Family in the Modern World), November 22, 1981.

_____. Apostolic Letter *Mulieris Dignitatem* (On the Dignity and Vocation of Women), August 15, 1988.

_____. Apostolic Letter *Tertio Millennio Adveniente* (On the Coming of the Third Millennium), November 10, 1994.

_____. Encyclical Letter *Centesimus Annus* (On the Hundredth Anniversary of *Rerum Novarum*), May 1, 1991.

_____. Encyclical Letter *Dives in Misericordia* (On the Mercy of God), November 13, 1980.

_____. Encyclical Letter *Dominum et Vivificantem* (On the Holy Spirit in the Life of the Church), May 18, 1986.

_____. Encyclical Letter *Evangelium Vitae* (On Human Life), March 25, 1995.

_____. Encyclical Letter *Fides et Ratio* (On Faith and Reason), September 14, 1998.

_____. Encyclical Letter *Laborem Exercens* (On Human Work), September 14, 1981.

_____. Encyclical Letter *Redemptor Hominis* (On the Redeemer of Man), March 4, 1979.

_____. Encyclical Letter *Redemptoris Mater* (Mother of the Redeemer), March 25, 1987.

_____. Encyclical Letter *Redemptoris Missio* (On the Permanent Validity of the Church's Missionary Mandate), December 7, 1990.

_____. Encyclical Letter *Sollicitudo Rei Socialis* (On Social Concern), December 30, 1987.

_____. Encyclical Letter *Veritatis Splendor* (Regarding Certain Fundamental Questions of the Church's Moral Teaching), August 6, 1993.

_____. Homily for the Beatification of Isidore Bakanja, Elisabetta Canori Mora, and Gianna Beretta Molla (April 24, 1994): *L'Osservatore Romano*, April 25-26, 1994.

_____. Homily in Baltimore (October 8, 1995).

_____. Letter to Families (*Gratissimam Sane*), February 2, 1994.

_____. Letter to Women (June 29, 1995).

_____. Message to the Second Special Session of the United Nations for Disarmament (June 7, 1982).

_____. Post-Synodal Apostolic Exhortation *Christifideles Laici* (December 30, 1988).

_____. Post-Synodal Apostolic Exhortation *Ecclesia in Africa* (September 19, 1995).

_____. Post-Synodal Apostolic Exhortation *Ecclesia in America* (January 22, 1999).

_____. Post-Synodal Apostolic Exhortation *Ecclesia in Asia* (November 19, 1999).

_____. Post-Synodal Apostolic Exhortation *Reconciliatio et Paenitentia* (Reconciliation and Penance), February 14, 1984.

_____. "World Day of Peace Message" (January 1, 1981).

_____. "World Day of Peace Message" (January 1, 1985).

_____. "World Day of Peace Message" (January 1, 1986).

_____. "World Day of Peace Message" (January 1, 1988).

_____. "World Day of Peace Message" (January 1, 1989).

_____. "World Day of Peace Message" (January 1, 1991).

_____. "World Day of Peace Message" (January 1, 1994).

_____. "World Day of Peace Message" (January 1, 1998).

_____. "World Day of Peace Message" (January 1, 1999).

_____. "World Day of Peace Message" (January 1, 2000).

Leo XIII. Encyclical Letter *Rerum Novarum* (On the Condition of Workers), May 15, 1891.

Paul VI. Apostolic Exhortation *Evangelii Nuntiandi* (On Evangelization in the Modern World), December 8, 1975.

_____. Encyclical Letter *Ecclesiam Suam* (On the Church), August 6, 1964.

_____. Encyclical Letter *Populorum Progressio* (On the Development of Peoples), March 26, 1967.

_____. Homily for the Closing of the Holy Year (December 25, 1975).

_____. Apostolic Letter *Octogesima Adveniens* (A Call to Action), May 14, 1971.

_____. Letter to the Fifty-First Session of the French Social Weeks. In *Le travail et les travailleurs dans la société contemporaine*, Lyons, Chronique Sociale, 1965.

_____. Message to the World, Entrusted to Journalists (December 4, 1964).

_____. Profession of Faith of the People of God (June 30, 1968).

Pius XI. Encyclical Letter *Divini Redemptoris* (On Atheistic Communism), March 19, 1937.

_____. Encyclical Letter *Quadragesimo Anno* (On the Reconstruction of the Social Order), May 15, 1931.

_____. Encyclical Letter *Ubi Arcano Dei Consilio* (On the Peace of Christ in the Kingdom of Christ), December 23, 1922.

Pius XII. Allocution (October 8, 1956).

_____. "Christmas Eve Radio Message, 1944."

_____. "Christmas Message, 1942."

_____. Discourse (October 29, 1951).

Pontifical Council for Justice and Peace. *The Church and Racism: Towards a More Fraternal Society*, 1988.

Roman Missal. Prayer Before Communion.

Sacred Congregation for the Doctrine of the Faith. Declaration *Iura et Bona* (On Combatting Abortion and Euthanasia), May 5, 1980.

_____. Instruction on Christian Freedom and Liberation (*Libertatis Conscientia*), March 22, 1986.

_____. Instruction on Certain Aspects of the *"Theology of Liberation"* (*Libertatis Nuntius*), August 6, 1984.

_____. Instruction on Christian Freedom and Liberation (*Libertatis Conscientia*), March 22, 1986.

_____. Instruction on Respect for Human Life in Its Origin and on the Dignity of Procreation (*Donum Vitae*), February 22, 1987.

Saint Augustine. *De civitate Dei.*

Saint Clement of Rome. *Epistula ad Corinthios.*

Saint Gregory the Great. *Evangelium Homiliae.*

Saint Irenaeus. *Adversus Haereses.*

Saint Thomas Aquinas. *Summa Theologiae.*

Vatican Council I. Dogmatic Constitution of the Catholic Faith (*Dei Filius*).

Vatican Council II. *Closing Messages of the Council.* "To Women," (December 8, 1965).

_____. Declaration on Christian Education (*Gravissimum Educationis*), October 28, 1965.

_____. Declaration on Religious Liberty (*Dignitatis Humanae*), December 7, 1965.

_____. Decree on the Apostolate of the Laity (*Apostolicam Actuositatem*), November 18, 1965.

_____. Dogmatic Constitution on the Church (*Lumen Gentium*), November 21, 1964.

_____. Dogmatic Constitution on Divine Revelation (*Dei Verbum*), November 18, 1965.

_____. Pastoral Constitution on the Church in the Modern World (*Gaudium et Spes*), December 7, 1965.

INDEX

–numbers below correspond to paragraph numbers

freedom of conscience (80, 83, 184, 270)
law written on the heart (53, 109)

CONSUMERISM (58, 64, 146, 161, 248, 249, 250, 298, 311, 316)

COOPERATION (27, 173, 195, 240, 244, 342, 345)

CULTURE (156–159, 250)
"culture of death/culture of life" (85, 105)
culture's attitude to mystery of God (160)
restoration of culture in Christ (155)
understand man within sphere of culture (160)

DEATH PENALTY (112–113)

DEBT
debt relief (347, 348, 361)
foreign debt (347, 348, 349, 361)
Year of Jubilee (347)

DEMOCRACY (58)
church's respect of democratic order (198)
importance of rule of law (182, 197)
moral value of democracy stands or falls with values it
promotes (199)
recognition of human rights (67)

DEVELOPMENT (see ECONOMIC DEVELOPMENT)
authentic development (40, 166, 360)
development of personal gifts (54)
economic development takes place over the heads of the
poor (291)
genuine human development (128, 141, 161, 165, 200, 294,
296)

work as vocation (253, 256, 257)

VIRTUE (289, 295)
    family as school of social virtue (84, 96)
    social virtues (240, 241)

WAGES (261, 262, 264, 267)
    free consent (265, 266)
    just wage (214, 258, 259, 263, 293, 327)
    wage determination (259)

WAR (330–334)

WELFARE (SEE SAFETY NET/SECURITY)
    rise of the "welfare state" (308)

WOMEN
    "new feminism" (117)
    real equality in every area (114, 116)
    work of women at home is irreplaceable (95, 115, 272)
    work outside the home (262)
    women's access to public functions (95)
    women who have had an abortion (110)

WORK
    connection to the image of God (251, 254)
    dignity of work (138, 215, 239, 241)
    the nature of work (251, 252, 268, 271, 285)
    work as creative activity (254)
    work as stewardship of talents (253, 255, 257)
    work as a means of sanctification (255, 256, 273)

WORK PLACE, THE (251, 261, 268–271)